# Outreach

Outreach

# Outreach

## Get Motivated to Reach Your Friends

**Don Babin**

© 2015 by Don Babin

All rights reserved. No part of this book may be reproduced, stored in a retrieval system or transmitted in any form or by any means without the prior written permission of the publishers, except by a reviewer who may quote brief passages in a review to be printed in a newspaper, magazine or journal.

First Printing

Publisher has allowed this work to remain exactly as the author intended, verbatim, without editorial input.

Ebook 978-1-304-62079-8

Softcover 978-1-312-82660-1

Hardcover 978-1-304-81830-0

**Published by:**

Revival Waves of Glory Books & Publishing
www.revivalwavesofglory.com
Litchfield, IL

Published in the United States of America

## Contents

Special Thanks ................................................................... 7
INTRODUCTION ............................................................. 9
*Chapter 1* MAD MAN EVANGELISM ................................ 21
*Chapter 2* FOLLOW ME ................................................. 45
*Chapter 3* RE-DISCOVERING YOUR TRUE IDENTITY 63
*Chapter 4* LIGHT OF THE WORLD ................................ 87
*Chapter 5* FALLING IN LOVE WITH JESUS ................... 107
*Chapter 6* ALL-OUT EVANGELISM ................................ 123
*Chapter 7* EFFECTIVENESS OF GOSPEL TRACTS ...... 141
*Chapter 8* CATCH AND RELEASE ................................ 159
*Chapter 9* SERVANT EVANGELISM ............................... 167
MY STORY ...................................................................... 177

Outreach

# Special Thanks

There are many people who have helped and sacrificed their time for me to be able to get this book in your hands. I am so thankful for these very special friends who have shown their love for me by their hard work and time.

Dotty Veralla, for reading and re-reading, and pointing out the many grammatical errors. She has been such a great friend and helper in this project.

Michael Washburn, for taking the time to draw our cover for the book. He is very patient. ONLY IF WE USE HIS COVER DESIGN

Carman Babin, a great son, for his putting up with his dad changing his mind so much. Thanks for helping me with the technology.

Michelle Babin, the best wife in the entire universe, who has patiently put up with me while writing the book. And for her years of faithfully being a great wife through the years of evangelism experience that went into this book.

EDDIE SMITH, for putting me in contact with the greatest publishing company ever. Revival waves of glory, has been more than a huge help. We love you guys.

# INTRODUCTION

It is my prayer that by the time you finish reading this book your thinking will have changed a little concerning evangelism. The word 'repent' simply means to change our thinking. It has been my prayer we repent about the way we think about outreach and evangelism. It seems to me the ones who still care about the lost are the new believers. Somehow in the midst of serving Jesus, we have lost the burden He has for those He came to 'seek and to save.' New believers usually make the best soul winners ever. It might be because they have such a burden for those they love who have not discovered what Jesus can do for them. The tragedy is they hang around those of us who have grown cold toward the lost and before you know it they become just like us. I am not sure why that is, but the new believers have much more of a passion for their lost friends then those who have been 'around church' for a while.

You would think that the longer someone has been around Jesus and His Word, the more he would want people to have the same relationship with Jesus. Those of us who have known the Lord for long periods of time should ask Him to restore us to that 'first love'. I know that we all want to be the kind of ambassadors that represent Him in a worthy manner. *"We are therefore Christ's Ambassadors, as though God were making his appeal through us."* (2 Corinthians 5:20 NIV).

A good restarting place is to take a good look at the importance evangelism plays in our lives. Does the importance evangelism plays in my life match that of the New Testament? Is the depreciation of evangelism a sign of our spiritual temperature? Is it strange to you that the longer we serve Him the more scriptures we can come up with to justify our actions? I know. I have been guilty of the same action. Let's allow the Holy Spirit to show us the truth and not try to cover up our short comings. The truth will set us free.

Please don't let this book be just an inspiration, but let it go deep inside of your heart and bring about a change in your thinking. We are not all called to be soul winners, but we are all subpoenaed to be witnesses. So let's get started by giving the Holy Spirit the right to show us where He wants to bring change into our lives. It wouldn't hurt to stop now and pray and give your heart over to the Holy Spirit. Say to Him, "I am open to your speaking to me about areas of my life that you would like to change."

When I began the journey of writing a book on this subject of evangelism, I struggled with the fact that books on evangelism don't have a large reading audience. It seems to me after serving God for over 35 years in full time ministry, I have seen evangelism take the back burner in the church. The church has moved away from soul winning campaigns to seminar and conferences. Seminars and conferences are important to the church and help us to grow spiritually, but so is obeying the Great Commission.

God called me to his miraculous salvation out of drugs and alcohol during the Jesus Movement of the '70's. I was amazed at how God set me free and gave me a purpose in life. He called me to the ministry of evangelism almost immediately. For 18 years my wife (Michelle) and I served God faithfully in full time evangelism. We planted an evangelistic church in East Texas and served there for 14 years. I have been on numerous mission trips and presently work with the Maasai Tribe in Kenya Africa. It has been quite an education traveling the world and sharing Jesus.

In my travels to hundreds of churches in the USA, I have heard time and again many reasons why evangelism is not a priority. I know for a fact this breaks Jesus' heart. Let me share just a few with you of the reasons why evangelism has fallen so far down the list of church and individual priority.

1. 'The evangelist of the past few decades has given us a bad taste of evangelism. They blow in, blow up and blow out'. As an evangelist I apologize for those who have been bad examples of the God given gift of evangelism. The days of the flashy colorful suit, flamboyant, fleshy approach has long been gone. We cannot judge the gift of evangelist by bad examples of evangelist.

Just like we cannot judge the gift of pastor by pastors who have been terrible examples of what a pastor is supposed to be. Many pastors have been hirelings, exploited God's people, had affairs, embezzled money and so on, yet I still believe in the God given gift of pastor. I believe this to the point that I am a member of a church and have a pastor myself. The same should be true of the evangelist and other gifted men given to the church (Ephesians 4: 11-13). We do not need to throw out the baby with the bath water. I guess the question we should ask ourselves Is, 'are the evangelist still a gift given to the church?', if so then how are we going to handle that truth. Is it possible that the church has moved away from evangelism because the church has moved away from the voice of the gifted evangelist. Just think about that for a while. We must have the voices of the gifted men given to the church.

11 And he gave the apostles, the prophets, the evangelists, the shepherds [2] and teachers, [3] 12 to equip the saints for the work of ministry, for building up the body of Christ, 13 until we all attain to the unity of the faith and of the knowledge of the Son of God, to

mature manhood, [4] to the measure of the stature of the fullness of Christ, 14 so that we may no longer be children, tossed to and fro by the waves and carried about by every wind of doctrine, by human cunning, by craftiness in deceitful schemes. Ephesians 4:11-14 ESV

We need to decide whether or not these few verses are true and apply to the church today. If they are true and do apply, it is up to us to work out the personal issues we might have with people and get back to what God wants for HIS church.

According to Paul, inspired by the Holy Spirit, the church will not, (1) be fully equipped to do the service God has call us to, (2) the church will not be equipped to build one another up like He intended us to do, (3) we will not attaint the unity of the faith or come to full maturity as He desires, (4) and the church will be tossed to and fro by every crazy doctrine available. This would be a great personal study if you want to see what God intends for His church by believing in and practicing the use of His gifted men given to the Body of Christ.

I firmly believe if the Church was hearing the voice of the evangelist we would not be in the terrible condition we are in today. The evangelist has a special anointing of sharing the Gospel. This is a message the church should never get away from. So many pastors are tired, worn out, burned out and getting out, because they have spent years trying to disciple lost people. This is absolutely impossible. I don't care how called you are, it is frustrating to try to get children of the darkness to walk in His light. It simple cannot be done. The evangelist has an anointing of calling out the lost. You have to be able to allow God to save those around you, who you were convinced were already saved. Many in our churches today, are tares that look like wheat. When the Holy Spirit convicts them that they are not saved, we cannot run to their rescue and talk them out of their salvation experience. In Matthew 7 many were deceived about their salvation and called God 'Lord', yet He told them He never knew them.

Now I am aware of those people who never come to the complete assurance of their salvation, but even then we must be careful to not interrupt what the Holy

Spirit might be doing. God is able to convince them they are the children of God, (Romans 8:16 'The Spirit Himself testifies with our spirit that we are God's children'.) God's spirit is quite able to do the convincing if we allow Him to. I know of a pastor's wife who gave a testimony that she walked the isle 4-5 times and each time the pastor would tell her she was already saved. Finally she said, she had to tell the pastors she was not and wanted to be saved. Basically she had to argue with the pastor to get saved. My point is, we must get out of God's way and not let our pride get in His way. I know we need to use the Word of God to help these people come to an understanding of what it means to be in a real relationship with God, but we must also understand it is a spiritual experience that is out of our control. Only God can save.

<u>One of the other reason I have heard evangelism is not a priority is:</u>

<u>We are struggling spiritually ourselves.</u> I had a group of leaders at a church tell me, that until the church was spiritual and rooted and grounded they could not be

a part of reaching other people. I was completely blown away. How in the world do you become a spiritual group of people when you live a life of disobedience to the Word of God and the great commission. It will not happen. Spiritual growth comes from being obedient. Could it be that the spiritual apathy, and lack of spiritual maturity is directly related to the lack of the DNA of the evangelist being imparted to the church and defiance of God's command to be a witness. Just a thought. During the Jesus movement we had a lot of bad theology, but we had a passion for the lost. Today we dot every 'i' and make sure every 't' is crossed theologically, yet we could care less about people going to a Christ-less eternity. Why can't we have both? If our theology is correct, we will be busy sharing the Good News. We need to be careful that we are not straining at gnats and swallowing camels.

There are so many other reasons I have heard. The purpose of this book is not to bash the Bride of Christ, but to be honest and build Her up. We live in a day when people are more open to the Gospel than any other time I have lived. God has set us up. 'The fields are white unto harvest'. The best time to reach people with the Good News is when they are facing a crises. God has put the whole world in a crises that we might go with the Gospel. People are afraid of terrorism, financial devastation, loss of jobs, foreclosure on houses, nuclear threat, not including personal pressures all this has put on families. I do not credit satan for being able to pull all this off by his own power. I believe satan's power originates with God. God has chosen to allow satan to bring crises that He can turn into good. With all this going on in society, people's hearts are searching for truth. We live in a day that people will listen to a believer if he is authentic. If the world sees we are real, and love them they will listen. I have been a soul-winner for over 35 years. Today, I have noticed people open to listening than any other time in my whole ministry. We as believers MUST take advantage of the open window of opportunity that God has set before us. If not the Scientologist, Jehovah false witnesses, Mormon, Muslims and other cults will take advantage of the times. I ask you to prayerfully consider what I have written in this book. I have written this book because we need more laborers in the fields that are white unto harvest. Please for the love of those who face a Christ-less eternity, let's do what Jesus ask each believer to do, GO!

Outreach

# Chapter 1
# MAD MAN EVANGELISM

There is an amazing story of four men and their aggressive attempt to get a friend to Jesus found in Mark 2:1-5. I cannot help but think these guys were the best friends a man could have in the whole world, because they were willing to do whatever it took. Now, that's what I call a great friend! By today's standard these men would be labeled 'mad men' especially when you see all they went through to get their friend to Jesus. By no means were these your typical church members. These guys were crazy for Jesus and knew He was the only one who could help their friend. Dwight Moody, the great evangelist, was called 'crazy Moody'. He would give free donkey rides to get kids to come and hear the gospel. Religious people of his day said he was crazy because of his actions, but he was willing to do whatever it took to get people to Jesus. These men were no different.

These four mad men were crazy also, but they were crazy like a fox. If I were a lame man and needed a miracle, I would prefer these four guys as my friends over anyone else in the crowd that day. I have included the scriptures here so you can read it yourself and not have to go get a Bible to look it up.

*"A few days later, when Jesus again entered Capernaum, the people heard that He had come home. So many gathered that there was no room left, not even outside the door, and he preached the word to them. Some men came, bringing to Him a paralytic, carried by four of them. Since they could not get him to Jesus because of the crowd, they made an opening in the roof above Jesus and, after digging through it, lowered the mat the paralyzed man was lying on. When Jesus saw their faith, He said to the paralytic, 'Son, your sins are forgiven.'"* Mark 2:1-5

Let's take a good look at what is happening here. You have four guys and they have a friend who is in desperate need of a miracle from Jesus. He has no hope of getting himself to Jesus and receiving his healing. Somehow, he has heard of this miracle-working Jesus. Imagine what went through this man's mind as he thought of those who Jesus touched and healed. Maybe he got a little hope for himself. Perhaps he thought, "If only Jesus would come to my town, maybe I could get a touch and be healed. Maybe, one day, I could have a testimony like others do." But then again, how in the world will he ever get to Jesus. I can't imagine knowing Jesus is going to be in town, healing other people, and yet having no way to get where He is going to be. So close to my miracle -- yet so far away. My limitations are going to keep me from receiving my miracle. This could be my only chance to be healed. Jesus may never return to town again. What am I going to do? The religious people hate me and believe I have a curse on my life because of my lameness.

How many people are so close to finding Jesus -- yet so far away. Their own limitations are keeping them away from Him. This is where you and I are to step up to the plate. Most people never find Jesus alone. If you read through the New Testament, most of the people who came to Jesus were brought to him by others. Our responsibility is to bring people to Jesus. Their limitations keep them from coming. These limitations could include fear, biased opinions, lack of understanding, laziness or just ignorance. We must make an effort to help these people come to Jesus. I believe that if lost people met the Jesus of the New Testament, they would do everything they could to get to Him. Unfortunately, the Jesus most people have met is not even close to the one I read about in Matthew, Mark, Luke and John. We must portray the TRUE Jesus if people are going to want to come to Him.

The Jews in that day believed that if you had a sickness it was because of your sin or your parents' sin. Therefore the Jews looked down on those who had some kind of sickness. Sick people were frowned upon by the religious people. Sick people were second class citizens. So this man had no hope of riding the church bus to Jesus. Who could he get to come and help him? If someone came for him they would then be looked down upon by their "church friends". After all, this man is a beggar and no good to society. He is rejected by church people and cursed because of his or his parents' sinful life. There is no hope for him of being healed. Only the healthy will be able to go to the church meeting Jesus is holding. Yet Jesus said, "I have not come for the healthy but for the sick." Perhaps they have not captured that revelation yet.

It amazes me how the church today is filled with people we think are healthy, yet Jesus came to the sick of this world. How many "sick" people are you taking to church? How many "sick" people do you know? These are the kinds of people Jesus came and searched for. Are you searching for them also?

Thank God this sick man did have four real friends. Without them he had no other way of getting to Jesus. Now the four friends knew what Jesus had done in the past, and when they heard Jesus was going to be in town at a home bible study, they all begin to plan. One thing that really stands out about these four guys is they had an unstoppable faith. They **knew** Jesus could help their friend and He was his only answer. We need this kind of faith. We need to know Jesus is the only answer for our friends. If we harbor hope for our friends apart from Jesus, we will not give an all-out effort to get them to Him. There is no alternative to Jesus.

The answer for the whole world is not a better job, good counseling (though I believe in good counsel), more money, a new car, a better wife or anything else. The one and only answer for the world is Jesus. When you and I really believe this, then, and only then, will we do all we can to get our friends to Him. We need more faith in what Jesus says than in the world's answers. Dr. Phil or Oprah do not hold the keys to eternal life. Only Jesus can touch a person in such a way as to change his entire life. Only Jesus has the miracle power to change a life and give true eternal purpose.

When the "mad men" heard Jesus was going to be in town, they begin to brain storm on how to get their friend to Him. They had, at the very least, to have decided when to meet at the lame man's house to take him to Jesus. Evangelism never happens by default--only by design. These four men had to plan on when to meet, how to get him there, and of course how to deal with the crowds that always followed Jesus. Getting their friend to Jesus had to hold enough of a priority for them to come up with a plan. We need to prioritize our evangelism. When evangelism is on the back burner it usually gets cold or just sits there and simmers.

When was the last time you had a brain storming session on getting a friend to Jesus? Churches all over our country need to have teaching on how to get friends to Jesus. I think it is very interesting that these men were not just thinking of themselves. They were not just making sure they had a good seat when Jesus was teaching. No way! They went way beyond a narcissistic Christianity. It was not about what they could get, or what they would receive, but instead about getting needs met for others. That is not a bad place for us to be. True Christianity is about serving others. When we get to the place that we believe all the songs we sing, believe it is all about Him and not us, we will begin to see the Kingdom of God come into our midst.

These four "mad men" did what they did because it was not all about them. They believed with all their hearts that Jesus was the only answer for their friend. Think of someone you know who has a desperate need. Can you come up with a better answer for them than to have a personal encounter with Jesus Christ? It never ceases to amaze me how churches have all kinds of strategy meetings on building buildings, developing better discipleship programs, better nurseries, or better presentations on Sunday mornings. These are not bad and many times they are necessary. My amazement is that we don't strategize as fanatically on reaching our friends as we do these other issues. If we would give evangelism equal time, we would have phenomenal success on reaching the lost for Jesus.

These friends were intentional about getting their needy friend to Jesus. It did not happen by accident or some sovereign move of God. Jesus sovereignly paid the price for our sin on the cross, now we must do our part. Jesus will not go door to door on our behalf. Worship does not just happen in our churches. Youth ministry does not just happen. Children's ministry does not just happen. You do not just happen to have a building where you worship.

These things happen because of a concerted effort of God's people. Evangelism is no different.

These "mad men" must have believed their friend was incapable of helping himself. He was hopeless without the help of Jesus. The lame man knew his need could not be met by man. This man put his hope in what he had heard Jesus could do. Thank God some people must have been talking about Jesus and His wonderful power. If people had not been talking, this man would not have heard and ultimately allowed his friends to take him to Jesus. When you have a person who hears what Jesus can do, and crazy friends that do not mind going to the extreme to get him to Jesus, you have a miracle waiting to happen. This man knew medicine could not help him. He was in desperate need of something beyond what man could do for him. This lame man trusted in his friends because they showed themselves worthy of his trust.

Getting our friends to Jesus is not always an easy task. Perhaps that is one of the reasons we shy away from it. It takes spiritual brain storming and tenacious praying. It takes someone who won't give up easily.

There is a battle that takes place when you attempt to steal people away from the hold satan has on them. He doesn't give them up readily. So if satan is not ready to give them up, and we give up easily, the devil wins. To get people to Jesus we must be willing to pay a price. Many times we have to get past our pride, peer pressure, lies of the devil, and much more.

The lame man must have had a great respect for his friends or he would not have allowed them to take the risks they did to get him to Jesus. He could have been made to look pretty foolish. It is critical that we live such a life before our friends and the world that they trust us. The world must see we have character and integrity. The world must see that we are trustworthy. We should be above reproach. Our light should so shine before men that they SEE our good works and glorify God (Matthew 5:16). Remembering that the world is watching us is a great motivation for living the Christian life. Let us never forget we represent or re-present Jesus and His Kingdom. The world does not read Matthew, Mark, Luke and John-- they read your life and mine. The only picture of Jesus they will ever see is how we live. We need to re-present Jesus to people.

We must live a life worth sharing and share a life worth living. I think it is our difference that makes the difference. When we lose our testimony we have lost the power to reach the lost world. Honest, Godly character, kindness and love are just a few of the things it takes today to impact and win the respect of the world around us (*Galatians 5:22-23*).

And now back to our story. The crowd became a major obstacle in getting this man to Jesus. Sometimes the very followers of Jesus hinder the needy from getting to Jesus. The church crowd can become an obstacle in getting the lost to Jesus.

Needy people may not meet the dress codes, or perhaps they look different, or maybe even act a little strange. But whatever the reason, if we are not careful we can become an obstacle to people coming to Jesus. In our story the crowd made it seemingly impossible to get the friend to Jesus. Surely they saw this lame man and his need for Jesus. Surely they saw these four men trying to get their friend to Jesus and not being able to because of the crowd. Perhaps they were so caught up with their own needs or just plain excited about hearing Jesus, that they became totally desensitized to other peoples' needs. I have been in churches where people get so excited about seeing their friends on Sunday, they never even see the visitors, much less extend a friendly welcome. I have met a lot of people who won't 'darken the door of a church' because the church crowd has so turned them off. We can become so enamored by the vision of the church that we forget that this whole thing is about reaching the lost for Him. Most of these people are not upset with Jesus, but our representation of Jesus. I love Jesus with all my heart and I get disillusioned by this kind of action. I find myself defending or protecting the reputation of the church… but the lost don't. They just take things at face value. Because of our personal flaws we hinder the crowd from coming to Jesus. This kind of attitude makes it extremely hard to win others to Jesus. It becomes an unnecessary obstacle we have to overcome to properly evangelize. We need to be the people that welcome those in need and lead the way for them to approach Jesus. This crowd in our story was totally unaware of the man's need. These four 'madmen', obviously, were the only men who brought a needy person to Jesus. It appears that no one else in the crowd even attempted to bring anyone with them. WOW, all the sick people in town, they knew from Jesus' previous visits what He had done, yet they did not go and get the needy. It seems to me that the 'meeting place' should have been filled with sick, needy people. But the opposite is true in our story. Instead, the house is filled with people who were not thinking of others. If we take the attitude of these four 'mad men' for Jesus, we will find a way to overcome whatever obstacles we may face when it comes to evangelism.

Not only do we have to deal with the crowd, in order to get people to Jesus we also have to deal with ourselves and each other. We have to look past our own disillusionments and obstacles and be totally focused on the task before us. Sometimes we have to look past each other's faults to work together. We must have our face set like a flint *(Isaiah 50:7)*. These four guys had an amazing focus. If we don't focus on the task of evangelism it won't "just happen". Remember, evangelism does not happen by default but by design.

The light in the room where you are sitting can be turned into an awesome tool. Just focus that light so much that it becomes a laser. A laser can be used to cut steel plate. We need that laser focus to overcome the crowds, our own personal quirks and other peoples' short falls. Evangelism can't be something you would like to see happen. It must be something you make happen. Just like these friends. These guys were focused enough to work together-- making sure their friend got to Jesus.

I have thought many times, what if this lame man had only one, two or even three friends. That would have made it more difficult for him to get to Jesus. The more people we have working together the easier our task becomes. If it is just you and two or three in your church bringing people to Jesus, you can do it. However, if you have more you will get better results. Evangelism is good discipleship. Evangelism will force you to work together and cooperate. These men had to strategize together. They had to make a plan.

When will we meet at a friend's house to get him to Jesus? I wouldn't be a bit surprised if these four men didn't already have a relationship. I am sure each of them had their own ideas of how to get him to Jesus, what time they should meet at the lame man house, what time to leave, arrive at the home Jesus was preaching at, and on and on. The point is they worked together to accomplish the task of getting their friend to Jesus. Proof of pure discipleship is how we treat one another. Jesus said, *"By this all men will know that you are my disciples, if you love one another."* John 13:35 (New International Version).

*"I planted the seed, Apollos watered it, but God made it grow. So neither he who plants nor he who waters is anything, but only God, who makes things grow. The man who plants and the man who waters have one purpose, and each will be rewarded according to his own labor. For we are God's fellow workers; you are God's field, God's building."* 1 Corinthians 3:6-9 (NIV).

The man who plants and the man who waters have one purpose. The purpose is to get someone to a relationship with Jesus. The method is working together. Now let's take a look at what happened that day. Walk with me to the village of Capernaum. Jesus is in a small home having a Bible study. The crowd is huge. People are everywhere. Some are standing inside and many are outside looking in the door and windows. They just wanted to hear what Jesus was saying. Not all knew Him. Some were there out of curiosity, some there to see if He was going to do one of His notorious miracles. Some were there just to be critical of the things he did wrong according to their traditions. There were all kinds of people there. Does that sound familiar or what? Sounds like some churches I have visited. Jesus is standing inside speaking. You could hear a pin drop it was so quiet and people were so attentive. Any noise would have been annoying because it would have made it harder to hear what Jesus was saying. Then on the scene come four 'mad men for Jesus' bringing their needy friend. I don't know if there was anyone else who brought a friend who needed Jesus, but no one else is mentioned. These four men who loved their friend came with a purpose. It wasn't just about what they wanted but about a lost friend. It seems to me if there were any other lame, sick, or demonized people Jesus would have addressed their need as usual. So I am assuming no one else brought friends with needs. This lame man was the only person who knew he had a need. I am positive others there had needs but they just did not know they had needs. Or their need was not as obvious.

What really captures my attention is the fact that the one man whose need was obvious could not get close enough to Jesus because the other people were in his way. My, my, my, how we church people can stand in the way of people coming to Jesus. What is really sad about this is we are not even aware we are in their way. You would think after the crowd saw the lame man they would have immediately made room for him to get to Jesus. Nope! They came to hear a good sermon, not to see people come to Jesus. This man's need never even crossed their minds.

If Jesus ever came to our town, we could at least walk to where He was speaking. But not this lame man. This could possibly have been his only chance to be healed. Maybe they never even thought of something like that. Wouldn't it have been cool if some of the people in the back would have said, "Hey guys move out of the way, make room for this man and his friends, this man's need is pretty obvious." That would have really impressed Jesus. Forget that! These people got there early and had their Bibles on chairs saving their seats for themselves and their friends who arrived late. But they definitely didn't make room for any other people.

Talk about a tough crowd. They were blinded by their own desires. If we are going to reach the lost we might have to forget about our needs and focus on the greater need. I firmly believe if we focus on others' needs, Jesus will automatically meet all our needs. Whatever we do, let's be careful not to become like the crowd on that day in Capernaum.

Whatever the crowd was like, it was not going to stop these men from getting their friend to Jesus. I love that kind of spiritual determination. They came with a plan and were not going to let anything or anyone stop them from getting their needy friend to Jesus. They made their way through the crowd enough to get to the roof's edge. They managed to get the man and the pallet to the top of the roof. I am positive they had some obstacles to deal with to pull that off. I would give anything to have been there and watched that feat. I can hear some of the ones in the crowd shushing them to get quiet. Their thoughts must have been, "How rude can people get. Can't they see Jesus wants to talk to us and these guys are bothering Him, right in the middle of a great Bible study?"

At the church I pastored, we were having a special when a man came in and sat in the back. He had a can of beer in his hand. Of course I was immediately told about this man and was asked if they should escort him off the property. As a matter of fact, the leaders who reported him to me were indignant about him doing such a thing. No one knew why he came to our service. It is important for you to know our church building was a former bar. As a matter of fact it was a strip club. Maybe this man thought the strip club was still there. But for whatever reason he came, he was in the right place. I told my leaders to just leave him alone and let him enjoy himself. For some reason I felt like Jesus already knew this man had come to church and had a beer in his hand. I am sure Jesus was not surprised like some of us were. I guess if Jesus knew he had a beer and was in church and it was all right with Him, why I should feel any differently. So if Jesus knew he had a drinking problem and came to church, who would he be hiding his beer from… Jesus or the religious crowd? Just a thought. I wanted him to meet Jesus and then his drinking problem would be taken care of. We don't ask people to clean up their lives and then come to church, but to come to church and let Jesus clean their lives up. AMEN?

I wanted him healed and saved and others just wanted him OUT! This precious man got prayed for that night. This man, so much like the needy man in our story, needed Jesus. The crowd however, was going to get in his way. But praise God we did not run him off to a bar, but left him in church and prayed over him. After the service we did hear a lot of religious murmuring about this man that came to our service drunk and carrying a beer.

*"An empty stable stays clean, but no income comes from an empty stable".* Proverbs 14:4 (New Living Translation)

We can keep our services so tidy and orderly, that we never see a harvest. Evangelism can be messy sometimes. But that's okay, even Jesus touched a leper to heal him. And that was against the Levitical law. But Jesus was not afraid to get in peoples 'mess' to see them healed. He could have shouted to the man, 'be healed', and he would have been healed. No, Jesus touched him.

We did not see any obvious change the night the man came to our service with the beer. One month later, however, he came again…but this time without a beer. He asked if he could share about a miracle God had performed in his life. I let him share and he said when he came to our service and got prayed for he left that night and God touched him. He had been a terrible alcoholic and heard about our church and thought if he came he could get some help. He was shocked we did not ask him to leave. He even said any other church would have run him off. That night God set him free of the bondage of alcohol. He had not had a drink since the last time he came to our church. This man got set free by the power of Jesus because we did not stand in his way of getting to Jesus.

In Mark 2:1-5, the crowd was not able to hinder these four men from getting their crippled friend to Jesus. They had to go to extreme measures. They tore a section off the roof of the house to lower him to Jesus. Sometimes we may have to take drastic measures to go around those who stand in the way. I am sure the dust and dirt were dropping all over the crowd and Jesus. It makes you wonder who He was impressed with the most - the listening crowd or the men who would do anything to get their friend to Him. When was the last time you saw a commotion over some people trying to get their friend to church to get saved? Or better yet, when was the last time you started a commotion over getting your friends to Jesus. Imagine being in a church service that is powerfully anointed. It was so strong people came from all over and crowded in the auditorium and outside to be a part. All of the sudden, you hear a couple of chain saws on the roof of your beautiful auditorium. To your absolute amazement you see pieces of the roof and ceiling falling on your beautiful carpet and the anointed guest speaker. The anointed worship service is being ruined. How would you feel at this point?

All of a sudden you see an opening in the roof. The stars are clearly visible. To your surprise you see four men lowering a pallet with a crippled man on it. I am almost positive that before now the men would have been arrested because you called the police. That is exactly why I call this 'mad man evangelism'. I am not suggesting we literally tear through the church roof to get people to Jesus, but I am suggesting we at least give it more effort than we do now.

What a great day that must have been for that lame man. I am sure he was eternally thankful for good radical friends. Because these four men made up their minds to get their friend to Jesus, no matter what, their lame friend walked home and is now walking on the streets of gold. Not only was he happy, I bet Jesus had the biggest smile on His face because one lame man walked due to the effort of these four good friends. Don't you just love the heart of this man's friends? If you and I could have this same attitude, that we will get our friends to Jesus no matter what, we too would see great miracles. What if you were that lame man? Which friends would you want? There are spiritually lame people at work with us, next door to us and all around us. Which kind of friend will you be?

Outreach

# Chapter 2
# FOLLOW ME

*"While walking by the Sea of Galilee, he saw two brothers, Simon (who is called Peter) and Andrew his brother, casting a net into the sea, for they were fishermen.* **And he said to them, "Follow me, and I will make you fishers of men."** *Immediately they left their nets and followed him. And going on from there he saw two other brothers, James the son of Zebedee and John his brother, in the boat with Zebedee their father, mending their nets, and he called them. Immediately they left the boat and their father and followed him."* Matthew 4:18*(bold and italics are mine).*

Jesus is actively looking for men who will become His disciples or learners. He happens to be walking by the Sea of Galilee and sees some fishermen, a common site on the Sea of Galilee. I am sure this was not the first time He had seen these same men fishing, but this was not to be just an ordinary day. After much prayer Jesus calls these men to follow Him and be His disciples. I love the way Jesus tells them right off the bat what His discipleship plan will accomplish in their lives. He clearly tells them that the result of following Him will be their becoming fishers of men. He did not say to them, 'follow me and there is a pretty good chance you will fish for men.' He did not tell them, 'follow me and you will most likely fish for men.' He did not say, 'follow me and I will try real hard to turn you into the kind of men that fish for men.' He said, 'the result of your following me is that you will become fishers of men.' You will become!!!! It seems to me that the result of being discipled by Jesus is that He will undoubtedly turn you into the kind of person who fishes for men. Do you see that? I don't want to put words in Jesus' mouth. Go ahead and read those few words that came out of Jesus mouth one more time.

***"And he said to them, 'Follow me, and <u>I will make</u> you fishers of men.'"***

You don't have to be a seminary graduate to read this passage and get exactly what Jesus is saying. Jesus said, 'following me will result in your becoming something. The result of your hanging out with me, being around me, listening to me, and watching me will result in your becoming a fisherman, but one who is catching people instead of fish. Before today, you have spent your life fishing for fish, after you have followed me you will fish for men. This is inevitable. It will absolutely, positively happen!'

A disciple was more than just a learner. He was an apprentice. When Jesus was looking for disciples, He was looking for someone who would learn from Him by listening to His words and by watching what He did. An apprentice learns by watching. Jesus was going to teach these men how to be like Him, and fish for men. He just exemplified this by asking them to follow Him. He was saying to these men, 'follow me and as an apprentice you will fish for men just like I did by fishing for you.' And then you will teach others what I taught you. We do the same today.

Jesus always does what He says. So, if Jesus said the result of following Him is becoming fishers of men, then the result of following Jesus will ALWAYS be 'fishing for men.' If you do not have the same consequences of following Jesus as the disciples did in Jesus' day, it is not that Jesus did not do His part. You and I becoming fishers of men is not about our giftings or our personalities. It is nothing less than just following Jesus. Too many people cop out of the end results of following Jesus by making excuses.

I believe in spiritual gifts and the motivations our gifts bring into our lives, but fishing for men is not about gifting but about 'following Jesus'. Our spiritual gifts will determine the style of fishermen we become, but we all will fish for men. Let me explain what I mean. If your spiritual gift is mercy, you will most likely fish differently than a prophet or an evangelist. A mercy-giver does great evangelistic work in nursing homes, hospitals, and among the homeless. A prophet does great in street ministry, and more confrontational evangelism.

A teacher flourishes in ministries of helps, like training others in finances or family, or even counseling using these opportunities to reach others with the Gospel. My point is--gifts are great to build up the body of Christ, but the motivation will affect how you fish for men. It does not matter what your gifting is, if you are following Jesus you will 'fish for men'.

Let's review the scripture one more time:

*"And he said to them, 'Follow me, and I will make you fishers of men.'"*

Without a doubt the result of following Jesus will always be 'fishing for men'. He said, "I will make you..." The responsibility is on Jesus. He will make us become fishers of men. It is up to Him to turn us into the kind of people who fish for men. He is not interested in 'making us fish'. He could do that if He wanted to. Since He is God, He can do whatever He wants. But in this passage He is talking about making us each into a 'kind of person'. He wants to make us each into the kind of person who *desires* to fish.

Understanding the nature and character of God, He gets no pleasure out of making us robots who evangelize whether we want to or not. He delights in turning us into the kind of people who have the same DNA as He has. He wants to impart to us the DNA that loves people and wants to reach out to them. By following Him, being with Him, and listening to Him He imparts His DNA—the heart of a fisherman. This is one of the major 'end results' of being discipled by Jesus. By being a follower of Jesus, His DNA will be imparted into us, and a part of that DNA will always be the ability to catch men. This is what apprenticeship is all about. A plumber imparts his style and skills of plumbing into his apprentice. They end up with the DNA of that particular plumber. But imagine if that same apprentice was born into the family of that plumber and watched his dad plumb and discuss plumbing his whole life. You and I were born again into the family of God, and we have the DNA of Jesus our teacher.

I have never been able to understand how we turn discipleship into anything other than what Jesus intended it to be. We may be uncomfortable with evangelism, we may not like evangelism, we may not believe in evangelism, we may be bitter toward evangelism, we may even resent evangelism, but the bottom line is this: if we are truly following Jesus we will get over all of these excuses. If we do the following, *He will do the making.* Jesus is able to do what He said He will do, if we are following Him. He has a plan. His plan is to disciple us into becoming fishers of men.

If Jesus' plan of discipleship is to turn us all into 'fishers of men', why is it that today most believers don't even think about reaching out to others? Could it be that we are missing out on the DNA that Jesus intends to impart to each of us. I am not talking about a program (though programs can help us reach people). I am talking about something spiritual that happens in a person's life when that person is faithful in following Jesus. That something spiritual will, without a doubt, happen in any person who is following Him. It can't help but happen, because following Jesus is our part, and making us 'fishers of men' is His part. Again, Jesus always does his part.

There seems to be a divine order of how God works throughout the whole Bible. I really want to be careful to not put God in a box. God is too big to reduce

Him to a formula. God does have His way of doing things, but He can always do things outside of His own box. So though I am going to mention a divine order on how God works, we must remember He can and does move outside of this order. It is called grace. Most of the time, if not always, God's order of 'doing things' in our lives is: 'when we do our part, He will do His part.'

The Bible says, *"Call to Me, and I will answer you, and show you great and mighty things, which you do not know,"* Jeremiah 33:3 (New King James Version). Here is God's order. When we call on Him (that's our part), He will show us great and mighty things (that is His part). He will do His part after we have done our part.

The Bible says, *"But seek first the kingdom of God and His righteousness"* (that's our part), *"and all these things shall be added to you"* (that's His part) Matthew 6:33 (NKJV).

The Bible says, 'Ask' (that is our part) 'and you shall receive' (that is His part). 'Seek' (our part) 'and you shall find' (His part). 'Knock' (our part) 'and the door shall be open' (His part). 'Give' (our part) 'and it shall be given unto you' (His part). We could go on for many pages, but the point is this-- if we do our part then He will do His part. We are saved because we did our part, 'whosoever shall believe in His heart, and confess with his mouth....shall be saved'. That's our part and His part. He will never fail in doing His part if we are faithful in doing our part. If we are faithful in doing our part and follow Him, He will do His part and turn us into the kind of people who 'fish for men'. There is no doubt about this. There is no doubt that He will do His part. The question is, and this is a hard question if we are honest with ourselves, are we really following Him?

Many people say they follow Jesus, yet the end result is not there. Now, don't get offended or religious on me. Conviction is a good thing; being offended is a bad thing. Ask yourself, "Am I becoming a fisher of men?" Ask yourself this question also, "Am I really following Jesus?" I think you see what I am trying to say.

If Jesus meant what He said and said what He meant, then when we truly follow Jesus we will become what He said we would become, which is 'fishers of men', AMEN? If we are not in the process of becoming what He said we would become (as a result of following Him), then is it possible we are not following Jesus? We may have great intentions, we may be deeply committed, we may be sincere but are we getting the results Jesus wanted as we follow Him. Is it possible we are following another Jesus?

*"I hope you will put up with a little more of my foolishness. Please bear with me. For I am jealous for you with the jealousy of God himself. I promised you as a pure bride to one husband—Christ. But I fear that somehow your pure and undivided devotion to Christ will be corrupted, just as Eve was deceived by the cunning ways of the serpent. You happily put up with whatever anyone tells you, even if they preach a different Jesus than the one we preach, or a different kind of Spirit than the one you received, or a different kind of gospel than the one you believed."* 2 Corinthians 11:1-4 (NLT)

Peter Lord, a great friend of mine, says, "You can win many ball games on the chalk board." God is not interested in us just getting the point or understanding what He was teaching. He is interested in us becoming who we are. A fisher of men is not just what a person does; it is who he is. If I fish for men, it is because that is who I am.

Is it possible that we could be deceived into following another Jesus? Could it be that we could be tricked into following an American Jesus, a Pentecostal Jesus, a

Republican or Democratic Jesus or some other Jesus other than the one we read about in the Bible? Could the reason we are not fishing for men be that we are not following the right Jesus? WOW! This could make some people really mad. It is my prayer that we don't get mad but we get broken. Maybe we will hear what Jesus wants us to hear. *"He who has ears let him hear..."* Matthew 11:15. Now don't go off and get so mad you don't finish the book. Just stop right now and pray. Let God speak to you. If what I am saying is true, GREAT, if not then read on. I am not sitting in judgment of anyone; I just want us to hear correctly what Jesus was saying. Did He mean what He said to the early disciples? Is it possible that in the midst of all of our religious calisthenics we somehow miss what Jesus wants us to become. It seems to me we have a whole nation of churches that are producing disciples who have no burden for the lost, no burden for those who do not know Jesus, and the result is we are losing a nation, and a whole generation is missing out on knowing God. When Jesus made disciples they became 'fishers of men,' shouldn't ours?

Let's take a look at what it means to follow Jesus. When Jesus said, 'follow me,' what did He mean?

**opisw mou** Greek--follow me means 'after me.' An invitation to take up an apprenticeship with the rabbi Jesus: "Here! Behind me," It is most likely that these disciples of John knew Jesus well and now that John had been arrested, were given the opportunity to serve the One John had pointed to.

**poihsw (poiew)** Greek future-- 'I will make.' Used in the sense of "cause someone to do something," (Cranfield) so "I will make you become in the future, after a course of preparation" (Grant).

**genesqai (ginomai)** Greek aor. inf. " [I will make you] to be/become [fishers of men]. The infinitive forms an infinitival phrase, object of the verb "make." The infinitival phrase is in the form of a double accusative construction, with the acc. personal pronoun "you," functioning as the subject of the infinitive, and "fishers of men" as the object of the infinitive; "follow me and **I will see to it that you become fishers of men**."

**ποιήσω ὑμᾶς ἁλιεῖς ἀνθρώπων** -- "fishers of men" - fisherman of men. "Fishermen who fish for men." When you put all this together you end up with, 'follow me, and I will make you into fishers of men.' He said, 'I will create, build or ordain you to become fishers of men.' Jesus is looking for people who are willing to follow Him faithfully, so He can impart His DNA--a heart that is concerned for those who do not know Him. Being with Him, enjoying His presence, learning from Him on a regular basis will ALWAYS result in us becoming what He wants us to be, not what we want to be.

He does not make us fish, but he makes us into the kind of people who 'want to fish.' There is a big difference. One is about 'law' the other is about 'grace.' *"Loving God means keeping his commandments, and his commandments are not burdensome."* 1 John 5:3( NLT).

'His commands are not burdensome.' When we love God the way He wants us to love Him, we will follow Him and have a willing heart to do what He teaches us. The lessons are not burdensome because we now have His DNA. Jesus did not dread reaching out to others. It was WHO He was, not just something He did. When we become who He intends us to be, doing what He commands is not a chore. Jesus wants us to enjoy who He makes us, 'fishers of men,' not dread it. The Christian life is not made up only of what we should be doing, but more so about becoming who we are by following Him and receiving His DNA. This makes Christianity so much more attractive to the world. We will look more deeply into this in the next chapter.

'Follow Me' is a very powerful command; a command that is much more an opportunity than a command. The disciples *"immediately left their nets"* Mark 1:20. They were willing to 'immediately' leave their nets, and everything they had learned, to follow Jesus because they saw it as an opportunity. When you hear the words from Jesus, 'follow me,' you should see an opportunity that goes way beyond anything you could ever imagine. Jesus, the King of the universe, the One who loves you more than anyone else, the One who knows you better than you know yourself, is calling you to be a part of His life, His Kingdom, and fulfill the purposes He has planned for you from the foundations of the world. Now THAT is what I call 'opportunity.'

The call to 'follow Him' is an opportunity for us and also for Jesus. His plan is to teach us to be fishers of men. Since we are 'disciples' or 'learners' He knows what we will become as a result of following Him. We need to be careful not to turn this calling into something difficult. Jesus said following Him, would be 'easy and light,' (Matthew 11:30). It is one thing for me to make myself a fisher of men, but it is quite another for Jesus to make me what He wants me to be. When Jesus does the 'making,' I find purpose and fulfillment. It is not something that is 'hard and heavy,' but 'easy and light.' The difference between what religion does and what Jesus does is the difference between 'easy and light' or 'hard and heavy.' Following Him is a great privilege, and the result of following Him is incredibly fulfilling. Jesus is looking for Ambassadors of His Kingdom. This takes some training. After years of pastoring, evangelism and now mission outreach, I have learned classroom education is not the best form for teaching or learning. Educators will even tell you that classroom education is the lowest form of education. The best way to educate is in small groups and role modeling. Perhaps that is why Jesus chose the 'follow me' method. By spending time with His disciples He was able to impart identity and not just a list of things that needed to be accomplished for Him. We will see this further on in this book.

Let me just briefly touch on what it means to 'fish for men'. A whole chapter will be dedicated to this later in the book. For now I want to clear up a major misunderstanding concerning evangelism. Many people think of evangelism as a rude, arrogant, insensitive way of telling people they will go to hell without giving their life to Jesus Christ as Lord. The truth is we all need to accept Jesus Christ as Lord of our lives and accept by faith His death and burial for our sins. We need to communicate this message to a world that is opposed to our portrayal of who God is and what God is like. I believe the world has not rejected the God of the bible but the Christian's portrayal of God.

To be an effective fisher of men we must be *"wise as serpents and harmless as doves"* (Matthew 10:16). We must be wise to reach our world. *"It is the goodness of God that leads people to repentance"* (Romans 2:4). By showing the lost world the love of God, the kindness of God, by being gentle, by being merciful, compassionate and caring we will see many more people turn to Jesus. Now we are on the same page concerning true Jesus style of evangelism.

Outreach

# Chapter 3
# RE-DISCOVERING YOUR TRUE IDENTITY

In today's world of technology we face the danger of having our identity stolen. Each year millions face the horrors that go with losing their personal identity. Anger, frustration, hate, fear, and worry are just a few of the emotions people feel. What is happening in the physical world is happening in the spiritual world also. Millions of believers have had their identity stolen by the lies of the enemy. This is more tragic than we could ever realize. This is something that is happening world-wide. It is amazing to me how many people have lost their spiritual identity and don't even know it. This is tragic.

Not only are these believers frustrated, angry, bitter, full of fear and more, but they are living by the lies the devil wants them to believe. It is impossible to live in the truth of who you are in Jesus, while accepting your identity from other sources.

When God spoke in the beginning and created the world, it happened. He said, 'light be', and it was (Genesis 1:3). His word was so powerful it had creative power. It still does today. When God speaks it is so. Our identity is found in what He says about us, not in what our parents might have said or are saying about us, or our friends, or teachers, or anyone other than God and those who agree with Him. If God says 'you are more than a conqueror' then what are you according to the word of God? Whatever God says is always the absolute truth. By faith we must accept what the Word of God says about us.

It is extremely important for us to grasp this truth in order for us to be all God has called us to be and to do all He has called us to do.

*"And this is the testimony of John, when the Jews sent priests and Levites from Jerusalem to ask him, "Who*

*are you?" He confessed, and did not deny, but confessed, 'I am not the Christ.' And they asked him, 'What then? Are you Elijah?' He said, 'I am not.' 'Are you the Prophet?' And he answered, 'No.' So they said to him, **'Who are you?** We need to give an answer to those who sent us. What do you say about yourself?' He said, **'I am the voice of one crying out in the wilderness, 'Make straight the way of the Lord,' as the prophet Isaiah said."** John 1:19-23.*

There are several things we need to see from this short passage of scripture. Let's take a look at what was happening. The religious leaders of that day had heard about John the Baptist. They had heard all kinds of things about who he was. Some had said he was a prophet. Some thought he was the Messiah. Some thought he was Elijah. What they really wanted to know is, 'Who are you?' They wanted to know what his true identity was. 'Who are you?' We must show the world who we are. The best testimony we can give to our friends and the unsaved world is walking in our true spiritual identity.

In the book of Acts, chapter 19, the seven sons of a Jewish high priest named Sceva tried to cast out demons like the apostle Paul. When they did, the demons spoke and said, 'Jesus I know, and Paul I know, **but who are you**?'

*"But one time when they tried it, the evil spirit replied, "I know Jesus, and I know Paul, but who are you?"* Acts 19:15 (NLT)

The world of the demonic knows the importance of us knowing our identity. True spiritual power comes when you and I knowing who we are in Jesus. The demons in Acts 19 wanted to know who these seven sons were. They knew Jesus and Paul, but these men had no reputation in hell. These seven sons were not known in hell as people who walked in authority. The demonic world knew these men did NOT know who they were in Jesus. That is why they asked the question, 'who are you?' What would you says if demons ask you, 'who are you?' If our light is going to shine brightly we must reflect Him. It is His light that guides the world. This is the light we are to reflect. When you and I walk in our biblical identity, we become light to a darkened world.

Understanding our biblical identity is crucial to having spiritual authority and to our being the 'witness' or 'light' Jesus calls us to be. The greater our understanding of who we are the brighter our light will shine. This takes faith. This takes <u>really</u> believing Jesus. This means taking Jesus at His word. If what Jesus says is true (and it is of course), then we must find our identity in what He says about us, not what family, friends, some preachers or others may say.

Perhaps you have heard sermons or teachings on this subject. Great!! To enjoy the benefits of this truth you must believe it, and let it live in your heart. Allow this truth to be incorporated into how you live on a daily basis. We live in a world where most people are programed negatively. We have all heard negative statements about our identity, like a parent saying, 'you will never mount up to anything', 'you are dumb', or 'you will always be stupid'. People have spoken curses over us: 'you are a looser', 'you can't do anything right', 'you are ugly', and on and on and on. According to the Word of God these statements about you are not true. These are lies from the devil. What is important for you and I is finding our identity in what God says about us. God is your heavenly Father and what He says about you is what counts.

In the New Testament there are over 300 identifying factors about who you are in Christ Jesus. Below I have listed just a few. Read over them, memorize them and believe each one. This is what your loving heavenly Father says to you and about you.

**The Word of God Says that in Jesus Christ...**

I am faithful (Ephesians 1:1)

I am God's child (John 1:12)

I have been justified (Romans 5:1)

I am Christ's friend (John 15:15)

I belong to God (1 Corinthians 6:20)

I am a member of Christ's Body (1 Corinthians 12:27)

I am assured all things work together for good (Romans 8:28)

I have been established, anointed and sealed by God (2 Corinthians 1:21-22)

I am confident that God will perfect the work He has begun in me (Philippians 1:6)

I am a citizen of heaven (Philippians 3:20)

I am hidden with Christ in God (Colossians 3:3)

I have not been given a spirit of fear, but of power, love and self-discipline (2 Timothy 1:7)

I am born of God and the evil one cannot touch me (1 John 5:18)

I am blessed in the heavenly realms with every spiritual blessing (Ephesians 1:3)

I am chosen before the creation of the world (Ephesians 1:4, 11)

I am holy and blameless (Ephesians 1:4)

I am adopted as his child (Ephesians 1:5)

I am given God's glorious grace lavishly and without restriction (Ephesians 1:5, 8)

I am in Him (Ephesians 1:7; 1 Corinthians 1:30)

I have redemption (Ephesians 1:8)

I am forgiven (Ephesians 1:8; Colossians 1:14)

I have purpose (Ephesians 1:9 & 3:11)

I have hope (Ephesians 1:12)

I am included (Ephesians 1:13)

I am sealed with the promised Holy Spirit (Ephesians 1:13)

I am a saint (Ephesians 1:18)

I am salt and light of the earth (Matthew 5:13-14)

I have been chosen and God desires me to bear fruit (John 15:1, 5)

I am a personal witness of Jesus Christ (Acts 1:8)

I am God's coworker (2 Corinthians 6:1)

I am a minister of reconciliation (2 Corinthians 5:17-20)

I am alive with Christ (Ephesians 2:5)

I am raised up with Christ (Ephesians 2:6; Colossians 2:12)

I am seated with Christ in the heavenly realms (Ephesians 2:6)

I have been shown the incomparable riches of God's grace (Ephesians 2:7)

God has expressed His kindness to me (Ephesians 2:7)

I am God's workmanship (Ephesians 2:10)

I have been brought near to God through Christ's blood (Ephesians 2:13)

I have peace (Ephesians 2:14)

I have access to the Father (Ephesians 2:18)

I am a member of God's household (Ephesians 2:19)

I am secure (Ephesians 2:20)

I am a holy temple (Ephesians 2:21; 1 Corinthians 6:19)

I am a dwelling for the Holy Spirit (Ephesians 2:22)

I share in the promise of Christ Jesus (Ephesians 3:6)

God's power works through me (Ephesians 3:7)

I can approach God with freedom and confidence (Ephesians 3:12)

I know there is a purpose for my sufferings (Ephesians 3:13)

I can grasp how wide, long, high and deep Christ's love is (Ephesians 3:18)

I am completed by God (Ephesians 3:19)

I can bring glory to God (Ephesians 3:21)

I have been called (Ephesians 4:1; 2 Timothy 1:9)

I can be humble, gentle, patient and lovingly tolerant of others (Ephesians 4:2)

I can mature spiritually (Ephesians 4:15)

You really are what God says you are. Think about this. If God says you are anointed, what are you? If God says you are righteous, what are you? Remember, whatever God says is true. He cannot lie. He is absolute truth. And the God of all truth says you are anointed, blessed, chosen, delivered, empowered, forgiven and much more. All you have to do is take God at His word.

The world will try to give you an identity. If you listen to the world your true identity will be stolen. As Christians we cannot find our identity in the world, even what our friends say or what our parents say. We must find our identity in who Christ says we are. Most of the world gets identifying factors from Hollywood. Your identity is not found in Hollywood, in your home, school, friends or business associates. Your TRUE identity is found in what Jesus says about you. Read over the list above one more time. Think about who is saying those things, and remember He is saying those things about YOU.

I understand it takes time to reprogram our minds to think like the Word of God and not the world.

*"Do not conform to the pattern of this world, but be transformed **by the renewing of your mind**. Then you will be able to test and approve what God's will is his good, pleasing and perfect will."* Romans 12:2

The discovering of our identity in Christ begins in our minds. We must have our minds renewed to the truth of the Word of God. If our thinking is programed like the world we will think like the world. We need to be reprogrammed to the truth of God's Word. The bible is true. Hollywood is nothing but a lie and a facade. If you want to walk in power, if you want to walk in freedom, if you want to walk in righteousness you must know what God says about you and add faith to it. Just believe God and what He says about you. You can trust Him.

Many Christians get their identity from how they feel. WOW! That is a fast way to depression. You cannot live by feelings.

*"The just shall live by faith."* Romans 1:17

Feelings are too fickle. One day you may feel really good about yourself, and the next day you may feel suicidal. One day you may feel like you and Jesus are best friends, and another day you feel like He abandoned you. That is no way to live in 'who you are in Christ Jesus'. Your identity does not come from how you feel about yourself. How does being righteous feel? How does being saved feel? I'm not sure we can really identify how these things feel. They could even feel different to different people. But life is not about feelings. If we make life about feeling good, we could be headed to drug addiction. I am not living to feel good. I did that before I came to Jesus and I was a drug addict. I am living to be the person Jesus created me to be. Our identity is not found in how we feel or in what others say about us. We must look in the Word of God to find our true identity.

Every day we look in the mirror to see what we look like. Before we go somewhere we take a look in the mirror to make sure we look all right. We know the mirror doesn't lie. Someone else may say we are having a bad hair day, but we want to see for ourselves so we take a look in the mirror. We would never get ready to go somewhere important and not use a mirror to see how we look. Imagine preparing to go somewhere and instead of looking at ourselves in a mirror we ask people how we look. We would never do that. We want to know the truth of how we really look. We don't trust people, not even our spouses. We have to make all the adjustments by looking in a mirror to see the truth of how we look.

*"But be ye doers of the word, and not hearers only, deceiving your own selves. For if any be a hearer of the word, and not a doer, he is like unto a man **beholding his natural face in a glass:** For he beholdeth himself, and goeth his way, and straightway forgetteth what manner of man he was."* James 1:22-24

James says the Word of God is our mirror. If you want to know what you look like you need to look in the Word of God. God says, *'you are more than a conqueror in Christ Jesus'* Romans 8:37. This is the truth about you. This is how you look in the mirror of God's Word. If God says you are 'more than a conqueror' then what are you? If God says, 'you are the righteousness of God in Christ Jesus' then what are you? You can trust God's mirror, it does not lie. You are everything God says you are. Add some faith to God's word and you will begin to walk the kind of life that God intended you to walk.

There are times in my life I don't feel like a conqueror. I may not even be acting like a conqueror. Others may be telling me I am not an overcomer. None of that really matters, because God says, 'I am more than a conqueror in Christ Jesus'. Even though I don't feel like an overcomer, act like an overcomer, and others say I am not an overcomer, I know what God says is true. So I look beyond my feelings, actions and what others say, and tell myself, 'I am what God says I am no matter what'. What God says trumps everything else. Nothing matters except what God says about me. I trust what

God says over and above my feeling, my actions or what others might be saying. God is always right. What God says is always the truth, no matter what.

Let's say you are sitting on your couch reading this book. The couch you are sitting on is green. What color is the couch you are sitting on? Green. Right? It looks green and everyone you know says it is green. If you could feel colors you would even say it felt green. By all facts known to your mind, what color is your coach? Green! If you asked the smarted most spiritual people you know they would agree with you the couch you are sitting on is green. Common sense, education, professional counsel, eye sight, discernment, every human resource would agree the couch is green.

What if by some strange occurrence God spoke to you and said in His Word and by His Spirit that the couch you have been sitting on is not really green. You have been taught by human vision and all other human resources that it was green, but now God is telling you that you had been advised and taught wrong, that the couch you are sitting on is not really green. Even you spiritual advisors had been wrong. Now, you have to take God at His Word. Even though it goes against all feelings, how it appears, what others have said, you must believe God. You now must take God at his Word above other people's word. Even a few believer friends agree with you that they learned the same lesson and the couch truly was not green. What if God said in His Word and by His Spirit that the couch you are sitting on is really hot pink.

Now let me ask you a question. What color does the couch look like? Green, right? Yes it looks green. What color does the couch feel like? Green, right? What color does the majority of your friends and educated advisors say it is? Green, right? But they are all wrong. Because what God says trumps everything. Now let me ask you, what color is the couch? Hot pink, right? Why is the couch hot pink? Because God says it's hot pink that's why. Whatever God says is true. It does not matter how I feel, what it appears to be to me, or what others say--what God says is always true. If God says the couch is hot pink, as far as I am concerned it is hot pink. God knows what is hot pink or green much better than I do. So I will not trust in sight, but I will live above 'see level' and accept what God says no matter what. If everybody I know says I am crazy, I don't care, I trust the Words of God over everything. If God says this couch that looks green to me is hot pink, then this couch is hot pink from here on. It is not hot pink just for now, but from now on.

Now, let me make my point. If God says you are righteous, what are you? *"For our sake he made him to be sin who knew no sin, so that in him we might become the righteousness of God."* 2 Corinthians 5:21 (English Standard Version)

The Word of God clearly states that Jesus was made to be sin, though He never knew sin, so that IN HIM (there is the key), we might become the righteousness of God. Now, according to the Words of God, what are you? You are the righteousness of God. Would you agree that means you are pretty righteous? You are the righteousness of God in Jesus Christ. YOU ARE, right now, the righteousness of God.

You may not feel righteous, you may not even be acting righteous, others may not be calling you righteous, but if God says you are righteous what are you?

Righteous, right? Because what God says about you trumps everything else. If God says you are more than a conqueror, what are you? *"No, in all these things we are more than conquerors through him who loved us."* Romans 8:37 (ESV)

According to the Word of God, you are more than a conqueror through Him. God clearly states you are more than a conqueror. So, no matter how you feel, what others say, what is going on around you, you are more than a conqueror. Why? Because God says you are. Again, you are what God says you are. His word trumps feelings, what others say or how you feel. You are, right now, 'more than a conqueror through Jesus.

We need to learn to accept God at His word. If God says the couch is hot pink, what color is it? Hot pink. Nothing else matters except what God says. Accept what God says about you no matter what others say, how you feel, or what is going on around you. God is always right, right?

Understanding all this, I can get to the point I want to make concerning evangelism.

*"You are the salt of the earth. But if the salt loses its saltiness, how can it be made salty again? It is no longer good for anything, except to be thrown out and trampled underfoot. "You are the light of the world. A town built on a hill cannot be hidden. Neither do people light a lamp and put it under a bowl. Instead they put it on its stand, and it gives light to everyone in the house. In the same way, let your light shine before others, that they may see your good deeds and glorify your Father in heaven".* Matthew 5:13-16 (NIV)

Please note that Jesus said, 'You are the salt of the earth'. He did not say go out and try to be salt. He was telling believers their true identity. I want you to say to yourself, 'I am the salt of the earth.' Think about who it is that is saying you are salt. It is Jesus--absolute truth. He is saying you are already salt. This is a part of your identity. We need to grab hold of our identity when it comes to evangelism. Jesus declares us to be salt but we must make the decision to be effective salt. Salt is only effective when it comes into direct contact with what is to be made salty. If I go out to eat a steak and would like my meat a little salty, I do not grab the salt shaker and put the salt shaker on my steak. If I did that the salt would not come into direct contact with the substance it is supposed to make salty. The salt is no good in the salt shaker. The shaker is just the container where the salt comes together. It is when the salt is out of the shaker that it becomes what it is called to be. You and I are called by the words of Jesus to be salty salt. Salt is only salty when it gets out of the salt shaker and comes into contact with the substance it is to change.

Too many times the salt refuses to get out of the shaker. We have many beautiful shakers that were established to salt their communities. Yet, we cannot get the salt to get out of those nice buildings and come into direct contact with those we are to effect. There have been times when I wanted to salt something I was fixing to eat, but the salt refused to come out of the shaker. The only way I could make the salt come out was to really give it a good shake. The church today must have a good shaking to get us out of our comfort zone and be who we are in Jesus. Remember, Jesus said, 'we are salt, we are light'. We are already these things but we are not fulfilling our identity, because we have focused on the 'shakers' and not the 'salt'. Jesus is not as concerned about how pretty the shakers are as He is about the salt that is remaining in them.

Back to the steak I was fixing to eat. Putting the shaker on my steak did not fulfill the purpose of the salt. Establishing a church in a community that needs the Gospel is not fulfilling the purpose by building a building in that community. Just as putting the salt shaker on my steak did not have an effect on my steak. We must get out of our buildings and be the salt that Jesus has made us. The whole idea here is not that we are or are not salt. The idea in this passage is being effective salt. Jesus made it very clear when He declared, *'you are* the salt of the earth'. We need to discover our identity as salt. Many Christians are spending their lives trying to become something God has already made them. If Jesus said you are salt (and He did) then what are you? Salt, right?

Once we discover who we are in Jesus the actions will follow. I can act like I am salt or I can just be salty. God doesn't want us to 'act' but to 'be'. We have way too many actors and actresses in the church already. God wants us to discover who we are so we will be who we are and not act. The word 'hypocrite' comes from a word in the Greek that means to 'put on a mask'. In bible days people would put on a mask to entertain the kings and leaders. God does not want us to wear a mask but to be who He has made us to be. When we do this we are no longer acting but being. God made us 'human beings' not 'human doings'. We can be busy trying to 'do church' when God wants us to 'be the church'. We can be busy trying to 'do praying' when God wants us to be 'a people who pray'. We can busy ourselves trying to 'act righteous' when God wants us to realize we 'have been made righteous'. Let's not give any more energy to trying to be 'salt' and just be salty. Let's not try to be 'light' but just let our light shine.

You are who God says you are. You are anointed, blessed, chosen, delivered, empowered, forgiven, healed and much more according to the Words of God. Just be who He declared you to be. When you get the 'being' down the doing just follows. Discover your true identity in God's Word and you will be who God has called you to be. Remember the verse we started this chapter with? When they asked John the Baptist who he was, He answered them with what the Word of God said about him. You are who God says you are. So let me ask you. Who are YOU? Your answer should be...

        I am anointed......

        I am blessed........

        I am chosen........

        I am delivered......

        I am empowered.....

        I am forgiven........

John the disciple called himself, 'the one whom the Lord loved'. Now that is a wonderful way to see yourself. To be able to say I am the one who Jesus loves. He did not say, 'I am a disciple or an apostle.' He was the one whom Jesus loved.  Finding your identity in who Jesus says you are is the beginning of real living.

# Chapter 4
# LIGHT OF THE WORLD

My wife, Michelle, and I go to Africa and minister to the Maasai tribe several months out of the year. On one of those trips I went with some of my Maasai friends to Mount Suiza. This is a mountain where the Maasai go and spend days praying. It has many caves underground that go for miles. To go deep in the cave you have to climb, duck, and crawl in some areas. Twists and turns are along the whole way. We had a couple of flashlights to show us the areas where we needed to turn, duck, climb and make our way deeper into the cave. On one of our stops in the cave I asked my friend to turn off his light and I then turned off my light. I cannot even begin to explain to you the thickness of the dark. It was as dark as dark can be. I could not even see my hand. It was a scary darkness. To think of walking just 5 feet in the darkness of that dangerous cave would be unthinkable. By turning around a couple of times you would not even know which way you were facing before you turned around. It would be absolutely, totally impossible to get out of the cave without light.

    Being lost in that kind of darkness would be terrible. Trying to move around would be harmful. Yet, people around us are trying to maneuver their lives living in darkness. Because they are spiritually blind and living in deep darkness, as they try to get around they are hurting themselves in terrible ways. They are stumbling and falling over drugs, suicide, hate, jealousy, envy, sexual impurity and much more.

    We made our way out of the cave and as we approached the opening of the cave we no longer needed our flashlights. The natural light took the place of what our flashlights had been doing. I learned several things that day in the cave.

***The effectiveness of the light is determined by the environment that surrounds it.***

When we were deep in the cave and we turned off our lights, we became desperate for the light. At the entrance of the cave the light was not needed due to the natural light and we could not tell if the lights were on or off. The darker the darkness the greater the light shined. As I looked back into the darkness of the cave I could not help but think of the millions of people who are lost and they are like people wandering around in the darkness of the cave. How terrible to be lost in the depth of the cave and trying to find your way out of such darkness.

*'You are the light of the world.'* The light is effective when it is surrounded by darkness. We need to shine where we are needed. I am so glad that someone came in the midst of the drug culture of the 60's and 70's and let their light shine. It was because of their light that I found my way out of darkness to Jesus. Each of us has a purpose. Jesus made us into light. Lights have a purpose--shining. We do no good shining in places where light is not needed. *'You are the light of the world'*. This is what Jesus said about you. The word

*'world'* is the same Greek word used in the bible when it says...

> *"Be not conformed to this 'world'..."* Romans 12:2
>
> *"For God so loved the 'world'..."* John 3:16
>
> *"In the 'world' you shall have tribulation....."* John 16:33
>
> *"Do not love the 'world' or anything in the 'world'....."* 1 John 2:15

There are many other references to the word 'world' in the New Testament.

'Kosmos', (Greek) includes the ungodly (unsaved) multitude, the whole mass of men alienated from God and hostile to Him and His Son Jesus Christ (See also Earth Dwellers, the synonymous term used by John in The Revelation of Jesus Christ). This meaning describes the system of values, priorities, and beliefs that unbelievers hold that excludes God. (E.g. Just mention the name "Jesus" in a positive sense in a secular setting!)

> *"You are the light of the world. A town built on a hill cannot be hidden. Neither do people light a lamp and put it under a bowl. Instead they put it on its stand, and it gives light to everyone in the house. In the same*

*way, let your light shine before others, that they may see your good deeds and glorify your Father in heaven.* Matthew 5:14-16

It is important to note that Jesus tells us where the light will be most effective. We are to shine in the dark places. We are to shine among the lost masses of people. We are to be in the darkness of the cave where light is most needed. Our identity is not in question--our location is. Jesus clearly states who we are: Light. The issue with Jesus is the effectiveness of the light he made you to be. Just like salt is only effective when it comes into direct contact with that which it is to change.

He even goes so far as to give an illustration of our effectiveness. "*Neither do people light a lamp and put it under a bowl. Instead they put it on its stand, and it gives light to everyone in the house.*"

The point here is the ridiculousness of lighting a lamp and hiding it under a bowl or a basket. A light hidden is still light, but it is a light that has no effectiveness. The purpose of a light is to help people who are living in darkness. Why would you light a lamp and then hide it so no one is benefiting from the light.

We are the light of the world. What good is our presence if we are not in places where we are needed? Our church buildings have become salt shakers and bushel baskets. Somehow our churches are now where believers meet and hide under their bushel baskets and shine, while they sing 'this little light of mine, I'm going to let it shine.' I am waiting for the Sunday when the church has a basket removal service.

Jesus goes on to state that when light is doing what it was designed to do it is impossible to hide. *"You are the light of the world. A town built on a hill cannot be hidden."*

Note the word 'cannot'. Jesus said when we are living out our identity and located where we are needed, we cannot be hidden. Wow! Jesus says it is impossible to hide our light when we place ourselves in the dark places of this world. There is no way to be in the darkness of the cave and turn on a flashlight and it not being seen. Impossible! People will see your light shine. People will see Jesus in you when you are in places where light is needed. You **cannot** be hidden. Just like a city on a hill at night cannot be hidden. Even today as you are driving in the country and approaching a big city you can see the light it gives off on the horizon. Even if the city tried to hide its light, it could not. You cannot hide your identity when you are in dark places.

The only way to hide the light is to put it under something. *"Neither do people light a lamp and put it under a bowl. Instead they put it on its stand, and it gives light to everyone in the house."*

We know from what Jesus said that you are light. No doubt about that! Perhaps you are not in a place where your light is obvious. The Kingdom of God does not need your light, but the dark world does. Go befriend someone who is living in darkness and let your light shine in his/her world. Or maybe, like Jesus stated, you are hidden under a bushel basket. There are so many kinds of bushel baskets for us to hide under. The bushel basket of fear, misguided teaching concerning evangelism, lack of love for the lost or getting used to living under a basket. Whatever our baskets are we need to remove them so the light we are can be seen by those who are lost in the darkness of this present world.

***The effectiveness of light is determined by the power that supplies it.***

Deep in that cave in Kenya, Africa, I couldn't help but think how good our batteries were. If the power source of our flashlights went out, we would forever be lost in the darkness of that cave. The light is only as bright as the batteries are strong. Have you even been in the dark and the light you used had weak batteries? The light it gave off was not very bright. Yet, you could put in fully charged batteries and it made all the difference in the world. A light with a full charge can make a bigger difference than a light with a weak charge.

*"Do not get drunk on wine, which leads to debauchery. Instead, be filled with the Spirit..."* Ephesians 5:18

The Holy Spirit is our source of power. In the book of Acts you read things like, *"filled with the Spirit they......" "But you shall receive power,"* When? *"after that the Holy Spirit has come upon you."* For what purpose? *"and you shall be My witnesses."* Acts 1:8

- Consider Peter's sermon in Acts 2:14-37. After being filled with the Holy Spirit, he preached.
- Acts 4--When Peter and John were before the Sanhedrin for healing the lame man they were on the spot. They were asked, *"by what power have you done this?" "Then Peter filled with the Holy Spirit gave witness to the rulers and elders"* (v.9). Yes, power to witness. Exactly what he witnessed is found in verses 9-23. After they boldly witnessed they prayed (see 4:24-30). What happened after they prayed (v. 31)? *"They were all filled with the Holy Spirit and spoke the word of God with boldness."* Being filled with the Spirit was for power to evangelize, to witness.
- Acts 6:3, 5, 7--The apostles chose seven men *"full of the Holy Spirit."* In v. 7 we learn some of the results of being filled with the Spirit: *"The word of God spread and the number of the disciples multiplied greatly."* I like that word "multiplied." This is another example of the connection of being filled with the Spirit and real biblical evangelism.

- Acts 6:5, 8--*"Stephen a man full of faith and the Holy Spirit"* (v. 5). *"And Stephen a man full of power."* (v.8) What did this man, filled with the Holy Spirit, do? The very next chapter, Acts 7, gives us the answer. He preached (Acts 7:2). He witnessed as to who Jesus was, and it was so powerful that it cost him his life.

- Acts 9--This chapter records what was probably the greatest conversion to Christianity--Paul's conversion. In Acts 9:17 we learn that Paul was *"filled with the Spirit."* What did he do immediately after he was filled with the Spirit? Acts 9:20: *"Immediately he preached Christ."*

- Acts 11:24--Barnabas was *"a good man, full of the Holy Spirit and faith."* What was the result of being "filled with the Spirit"? *"And a great many people were added to the Lord."* (Acts 5:14; 11:21.) Barnabas was empowered to evangelize.

There are other references in the Book of Acts to "being filled with the Spirit." Any careful study will clearly show that the filling of the Spirit was to give power for gospel purposes and to empower the apostles to do unusual things to authenticate and confirm their message.

The effectiveness of our light is determined by the power that supplies it. We are commanded to "*be filled with the Spirit*". God has empowered us that we might walk in who we are. God's word clearly declares who we are. God's word is the mirror of our true identity. The Holy Spirit is the power source for us to walk in who we are. It was very important to Jesus that the disciples go to Jerusalem before they fulfilled the commissioning they received from Jesus to 'GO'. It was so they would be filled with the Spirit. We must be filled with the Spirit to fulfill our calling and to walk in our identity. The Holy Spirit is the "batteries" for the light. Keep a full charge on the batteries and you will shine brightly in a dark world. A light is a light -- and you are light. The only difference is how brightly you shine.

I have learned over the years that whatever fills my life is what comes out of my life. Imagine my having an empty glass and a pitcher fill of water. If I begin to pour water from the pitcher into the empty glass, how will you know when it is full? If I filled the glass until it was just one inch from the top, would you call the glass full? Of course not. If I filled the glass until it was very close to the top, would you call the glass full? No not really. But if I kept pouring water from the pitcher, at what point would you tell me to stop pouring because the glass was full? Answer....when it started to overflow. When the water started coming over the edge, you would say it is full.

People can tell when we are full of the Holy Spirit because we overflow with whatever fills us. In the world the devil is going to thump us. He is going to come along and try to rock our world. If the devil does not cross our path, we need to be careful we are not walking with him. When he does thump us, whatever fills our life is what will come out. For example: if the glass is full of water and I thump it, water comes out of the glass. If the glass is full of lemonade and I thump the glass, lemonade will come out. Why? Because whatever fills the glass is what comes out. If you are filled with anger, hate, or depression and the devil thumps your life, the only thing that can come out is anger, hate or depression. If the devil thumps your life and you are filled with the Holy Spirit then the Holy Spirit will come out.

Our goal is to shine brightly on people who live in darkness. Let the Holy Spirit fill your life and then you will have the power to shine brightly to those lost in darkness. To walk full of the Holy Spirit, you will need to get refilled every time the devil thumps your life. When the devil thumps you and the Holy Spirit comes out, you need to refill those areas of your life. This is why the bible says in Ephesians 5:18 (according to the Greek translation), *"be continually filled with the Spirit"*. We must have the Spirit continually flowing into us, so when the devil thumps us we stay full.

***The effectiveness of the light is determined by the cleanliness of the lens.***

The cave in Africa was very dusty. It was like a heavy powder several inches think on the cave floor. After crawling around and climbing, the lens of the light would become covered in dust. While making our way through the cave we did not notice the lens of the flashlight being covered by dirt and dust, but the further we went into the cave the light got dimmer and dimmer.

It happened in such a slow manner we did not even recognize the light getting dimmer. It does not take a lot of light to make a difference when you are surrounded by thick darkness. We were so thankful for the light we had we did not notice the dirty lens had dimmed our lights.

As we make our way in this world, we pick up the dirt and the dust of life. This is hard to even notice. A little compromise here and a little there and before you know it, our lights have become dim. I don't say this for us to feel condemned, but to make us aware of how the world can affect us. Awareness is the biggest part of our battle. Living in denial can become our biggest enemy. The enemy never steals our heart in a day or two. He is patient. He will take his time stealing a small part of our heart at a time until one day we realize we have slipped far away from the deep personal relationship with Him we enjoyed so much.

*"God made him who had no sin to be sin for us, so that in him we might become the righteousness of God."*
2 Corinthians 5:21 (NIV)

Because of Jesus' death on the cross we have been made the righteousness of God. That is pretty righteous. As a matter of fact that is as righteous as a person can become. Our righteousness is not about us but about His declaration over us. If Jesus says we are 'righteousness' then what are we? Righteous! So how does all of this fit? If God declares me to be righteous, and my lens becomes dirty, and my light becomes dim, am I still righteous? Yes, an emphatic yes! Once we have come into the family of God, by faith through grace, we are what Jesus declares us to be. It may be that we are not walking in all that He desires we walk in but we are still what He declares. As I stated in the previous chapter, as we realize our identity, and embrace who God declares us to be, the doing becomes easier. I walk in who I believe I am.

When someone is saved, that person is justified by God. Justified mean to be made 'just as if' I had not sinned. We do not have time to go into the doctrine of justification, but this would be a great study for you to do on your own time. Also as a part of your salvation you are being sanctified. This is the process of us becoming all God wants us to be. Justification is immediate and sanctification is a process. We are in the process of being conformed into the image of Jesus Christ (Romans 8:29). This process is not a process of us living under condemnation, *"There is therefore now, no condemnation to those who are in Christ Jesus"* Romans 8:1. God wants us to be conformed to the image of Jesus. We are being conformed in our minds, *"Be not conformed to this world but transformed by the renewing of your minds"* Romans 12:2. The renewing of our minds takes time. Some people take longer than others. The whole idea here is for us to become more like Jesus so our lights will shine brightly and the world will come to Jesus. The more we cooperate with God in making us more like Jesus the more we enjoy our relationship. The more we enjoy or relationship the more people will desire what we have. Remember, we are the salt of the earth. Salt makes people thirsty. We should have such a peace with God and enjoy our relationship with Him so much that people who see us get thirsty for what we have. We are the 'ambassadors of God'. We should re-present Jesus (or represent Him) in such a way, that we become a God magnet.  The more we cooperate with God in becoming the image of Jesus the more we draw people to Jesus and not away from Him.

This is my point!  You need to accept who you are in Jesus, allow the Holy Spirit to show you the areas of your life that are not like Jesus, and then cooperate with Him conforming you to become more like Him.  The world has a way of making our lenses become dusty and dirty.  The blood of Jesus cleanses us from all sin (1 John 1:9).  Simply ask Jesus to cleanse your lens from those things that dim your light.  It really is that simple.  He delights in forgiving you.  He delights in cleansing your lens so that you can shine brighter for Him.

This world has a way of just sticking to us.  Imagine your life being like fly paper.  Have you ever seen fly paper?  It is that real sticky strip of yellow paper that you hang up and when a fly touches it, the fly gets stuck for life.  As we go through this life the things of the world stick to us like our life was fly paper.  There are a lot of things in the world that set us up for failure.  The only way to be able to walk through this world and not have things stick is to take the fly paper and dip it in oil.

That's right, dip it in oil. Oil is symbolic of the Holy Spirit throughout scripture. So if we allow God to dip our lives into the Holy Spirit, all of a sudden the sticky loses it power. The power of the Holy Spirit will take away the power of sin to stick in our lives and cause us to live a life of victory and power.

In the cave, the lens just needed to be wiped clean and the light would shine much brighter. *"If we confess our sin, He is faithful and just to forgive our sin and CLEANSE us from all unrighteousness."* 1 John 1:9

Just ask Him to cleanse you and the lens will be made clean so your light will shine. Then others will see your good works and glorify your father who is in heaven.

*"In the same way, let your light shine before men, that they may see your good deeds and praise your Father in heaven."* Matthew 5:16 (NIV)

I really like this verse. I like the part that says, *"that they may see"*. That who may see? Obviously it's the people who need light, those who are lost in the deep darkness of the world. God wants us to live a clean life so that others can see.

Today, why not live this little tune I use to sing when I gave my heart to Jesus in the early 70's?

*"This little light of mine, I'm going to let it shine. This little light of mine, I'm going to let it shine. This little light of mine, I'm going to let it shine. Let it shine, let it shine, let it shine."*

Outreach

# Chapter 5
# FALLING IN LOVE WITH JESUS

You cannot motivate people to be involved in reaching out to others by preaching evangelism, but if people fall in love with Jesus they will automatically care about others. The greatest motivation for evangelism is a great love for Jesus.

*"For this is the love of God, that we keep his commandments. And his commandments are not burdensome."* 1 John 5:3

*'And His commands are not burdensome'.* Wow! I like that a lot. His commands are not hard. Jesus said, *'learn from me, for my yoke is easy and my burden is light'.* "And his commandments are not grievous." Matthew 11:30 (Greek: heavy--\~bareiai\~; that is difficult to be borne as a burden).

Religion has always handed down commandments of men, but not of God. These commands are hard and create burdens for people that even those who teach such commands do not follow them.

*"They worship me in vain; their teachings are but rules taught by men."* Matthew 15:19 (NIV)

Religion has a history of manipulating people into fulfilling what the leaders of that religion have wanted to fulfill. Religion is not about relationship but about rules. Religion is not about loving people but about loving agendas. On the other hand, loving Jesus is about relationship. If the relationship is right the rules are no problem. If we focus on the rules and not on deepening our relationship with Jesus we end up being as religious as the Pharisees of Jesus day. Wearing the yoke of religion is hard and heavy but yoking up with Jesus is easy and light (Matthew 11:30).

Jesus was constantly reminding us that love was His main focus.

*"Teacher, which is the greatest commandment in the Law? Jesus replied: Love the Lord your God with all your heart and with all your soul and with all your mind. This is the first and greatest commandment. And the second is like it: Love your neighbor as yourself. All the Law and the Prophets hang on these two commandments."* Matthew 22:36-40

The New Covenant is full of encouragement to love one another, to love God, and how love was the most important factor of following Him. How we get away from this fundamental truth, I do not know. If love is our focus, everything else will fall in place. Jesus came to reach the world with the Gospel because He SO loved the world. John 3:16. When we SO love the world (the lost masses of people), we will have the proper desire to reach the world with the Gospel also.

Love is the greatest motivation to outreach, but it is also the key to effective outreach. Someone has said, 'people don't care about how much you know until they know how much you care'. When people see how much we care about them and love them, they realize we are not just fulfilling our religious obligations but are genuine and authentic in what we are doing. This is so important if we want to be effective in reaching people for Jesus.

People who do not know Jesus can see right through our religious ways. They can also see when we are being real. Whether it is at a restaurant trying to reach the waiter or waitress, or at the grocery story, people can tell if we really care. Imagine being at a restaurant with some friends and you want to reach the person serving you that evening. First and foremost you must never embarrass them or be rude to them. Treat them like they were your mom or own son or daughter working there. Just be nice and loving. These two things should be very easy for a Christian. Most servers have a name tag on their clothes. From the very beginning use their name when you converse with them. People love to hear their name and it also makes it very personal. If they do not have a name tag ask their name and use it.

Be real, yet have joy. Don't re-present Jesus as some dull, sad, depressed Jesus and Christianity as some unhappy way of life. Let them see Jesus as He is in the New Testament. Let them see the Jesus who had great joy. Let them see that Christianity is fun and not boring. You may have to make this a conscience effort until it is who you are. You may have to 'faith it' at first. Why not? We 'faith' our worship sometimes. We 'faith' our giving sometimes. Why not 'faith' our witness sometimes. First apply faith, then it will become who you are.

When someone really loves Jesus it shows. Have you ever heard someone say, "Wow, that person really loves Jesus a lot?" They said that because it showed.

There were things about that person that showed they loved Jesus with a great love. Are people saying that about us?

Are people saying that it is obvious you love Jesus a lot? If not, why not? I think love for Jesus is very evident. When someone loves Jesus it cannot be hidden. *This little light of mine, I'm gonna let it shine.* The light is the love of Jesus and our love for Jesus. I do not think you can pretend to love Jesus, at least not for a long period of time. When it is real, it shines forth. This whole Jesus thing can be put into commands. Love God a lot, love people a lot. It's just that simple.

The first and greatest command was not to just love God. Read it again for yourself.

*"Teacher, which is the greatest commandment in the Law? Jesus replied: Love the Lord your God with all your heart and with all your soul and with all your mind. This is the first and greatest commandment. And the second is like it: Love your neighbor as yourself. All the Law and the Prophets hang on these two commandments."* Matthew 22:36-40

After reading those verses, does it simple say to love God or to love Him a certain way. I know people who are not born again and will argue the whole way to hell that they love God. Maybe they are a part of a cult or a church that does not preach being born again. How many people do you know who love God the way He wants us to love Him. He said, *"Love Me with all your heart, soul and mind."* He is saying I want you to be consumed with loving me. Why is this so important?

Because Christianity is not about rules--but about relationship. It is all about relationship. When we love God the way He wants us to love Him, we will have the proper relationship that causes us to shine. When we love God this way, we will automatically love people the same way.

I remember in the '80's there was an acrostic going around that told people what real joy was. JOY stood for **J**esus, **O**thers and **Y**ou. If you put Jesus first, then others, and you last, you will discover real joy. That is so true. Today most people think we are supposed to be first, then Jesus then others. This is the fast track to a religious spirit.

I have discovered the more you love Jesus the easier it is to tell people about Him. When you love Jesus and are consumed by you relationship with Him and love others the same way, outreach become natural. Outreach is the outcome of true love. Yet today so few churches are involved in reaching their communities. Perhaps the problem is not outreach but we are too in love with ourselves.

I love my wife Michelle. No one has to twist my arm for me to brag on what a great wife and person she is. When I go somewhere and she is not there, I always talk about her. Not because I have to, but because I love her so much. Imagine me talking about my wife because that is what good husbands do and not because I love her and want to talk about her. Imagine me talking about her because that is what you are supposed to do when you are married, but not because I am crazy in love with her. What if I only talk about her because I want to be like other good husbands, this would really break my wife's heart.

There is a big difference in talking about Jesus because we are crazy in love with him and because it is just the right thing to do or I am obligated to. Whatever we love a lot, we talk about a lot. When you meet someone who loves football a lot, football will eventually become a part of their conversation. Jesus put it this way, "out of the abundance of the heart the mouth WILL speak." Luke 6:45 When Jesus fills our hearts, our mouths will talk about Him. Once we have a passion for Jesus the compassion for people will follow.

The people whom I have met who obviously love Jesus with a big love always have certain characteristics. It is these characteristics that make it plan they love Jesus in a very special way. Below I have listed some of the traits of the people whom I have met who simply cannot hide their great love for Him.

**1. They enjoy God.** The writers of the Westminster Confession, written in the 17th century, put it this way:

"The chief end of man is to *glorify God, and to enjoy him forever.*"

One thing is sure--the writers of the Westminster Confession understood how to keep the main thing the main thing. They said: *our chief end is to 'glorify God and <u>enjoy Him forever</u>'*. Someone said, "It would make a lot more sense to say, 'our chief end is to glorify God BY enjoying Him forever." I like that. God gets great glory when people see how much we enjoy Him.

Many people fear God in an unhealthy way. This is a terrible witness to people who do not yet have a relationship with Him. When people see how much we enjoy our relationship with Him, it becomes a great way to reach others. I have often wondered about the image of God that we, as believers, have given the world. Have we sent the world the wrong image of God? I know if most people meet the Jesus of scriptures they would be drawn to Him and would want to have a personal relationship with Him. Mahatma Gandhi once said, "If it were not for the Christians I knew I might have become one." I wonder how many people we know who are saying the same thing. God is not half as mean as a lot of believers portray Him. I don't know about you but I truly enjoy my relationship with God. I enjoy talking to Him in prayer, telling others about His goodness and mercy and the benefits of knowing Him. Perhaps we need a truer image of the Jesus from scriptures. Then we could all enjoy Him so much more than we do.

Imagine what the church would be like if all believers enjoyed God immensely: worship would be different, evangelism would be more effective, giving would be more enjoyable, church would be more life changing. One thing for sure, the people whom I have meet who love Jesus in a huge way really enjoy their relationship with Jesus. They talk about Him freely with their friends. They have a kind, gentle and sensitive way of sharing Jesus with others. They know the right things to say at the right time. I have been with people who share Jesus with others and I have been totally embarrassed. I have even wanted to apologize for the way they witnessed to others.

I want the world to know I am having the best time of my life serving Jesus. Have you ever been around believers who looked like they had the flu? I have and it is embarrassing. As believes our demeanor should show that we are enjoying God. When the world sees that we enjoy serving God they will begin to investigate what we believe. It might be a helpful thing to start your day with a prayer, and ask God to teach you how to enjoy Him daily. Everybody is different. How you show your enjoyment of Him will be different from how I, or someone else, enjoy Him. Still, the enjoyment should be seen by others. Go out today and enjoy the personal relationship you have with the God who sent His son to bring you and Him into a deep personal relationship. He really does love you all day long. Enjoy Him!

2. **They have a realness about them.** The people I know who have a reputation of 'just loving Jesus' come across as so authentic. They don't seem to wear their phylacteries so long that everyone can see them. They don't need to pray in public so everyone can hear them. They don't seem to witness to other just for the sake of a show. But they have a genuine love for people because they love Jesus so much.

It is real and not fake or religious. Jesus said, *"Beware of the leaven of the Pharisees."* Matthew 16:11-12. What was Jesus warning us about?

Jesus knew the danger of the teachings of the Pharisees. It was so easy in His day to fall into following a list of rules and missing out on the presence of Jesus. That danger lives today. Remember, it only takes a little leaven to take over the whole loaf. If we keep the main thing the main thing, this will take care of itself. If you and I focus on loving Jesus the way He wants to be loved, He will protect us from all the little fox's that destroy the vineyard (Song of Solomon 2:15). Jesus did not create us to be robots but to be people who love walking with Him through the cool of the garden. We need to enjoy our relationship with Him and not get all hung up on the rules religion has put on our shoulders. Religion separates and divides, but relationships restore and refresh.

People who love Jesus seem to have a 'freshness' about them. They live off their intimacy with Jesus and not off some religious experience. They walk with Him, and talk with Him along life's narrow way. I really appreciate those I walk with who have a contagious love for Jesus. Being with them makes me want to have what they have. They don't try to come across as perfect or holy, but it is so evident that they have something real special with Jesus. We can all have that and should. We all need to be contagious with the love of Jesus.

3. **They have an infectious joy.** Believers who love Jesus with that 'all out' kind of love have a joy about them that is unspeakable and full of glory! (Peter 1:8). I don't think I have ever met anyone who is full of the love of Jesus who lives in depression or walks around like

they have the flu.  Why in the world do so many believers live like they need a therapist?  I believe it is because they have left their first love (Revelation 2:4).  This is a passage where Jesus commends the church for being devoted, determined, and dedicated.  Yet Jesus has a great thing against them.  There was something in this church that disturbed Jesus greatly.  They had left their first love.  They did not lose it.  There is a big difference in losing something and leaving it.  If you lost it, you do not know where it is.  If you left it somewhere you simple have to go back to where you left it.  It seems to me that many believers need to find where they left their first love for Jesus.  Was it left in the success you had in business?  Was it left in the busyness of life?  Where did we leave our first love for Jesus?  In other words, do we love Jesus more today than we did when we first met Him?  Or have we lost our passionate love for our savior?  That first love is the love that causes someone to have an infectious joy for Jesus.

    I remember when I first fell in love with Michelle.  All I could think about was how much I loved her.  I loved her so much my 3.87 GPA fell way down.  I had a hard time thinking of anything else but her. I talked about her to anyone and everyone. I was always showing her picture to my friends and telling them about her. Why? Because I loved her so much. My friends even said I walked around in a daze. I smiled all the time before I met her, but now I smiled so big my face hurt. I had such joy that I met the love of my life.

When we give our hearts and lives to Jesus we do this because of a new found love. We are excited about our new journey with Him. We discover the joy of the Lord, which is a fruit of His Spirit. This kind of person becomes infectious with the joy and passion of Jesus. Evangelism is showing the love of Jesus with a joy that is so infectious people want to get in on it. I gave my life to Jesus because a friend of mine who met Jesus and showed the joy of the Lord in his life. I was desperate to have the joy he showed. His joy was like the salt of the earth that made me thirsty for Jesus.

Are we making people thirst for Jesus by the joy we show? You cannot work up this kind of joy. This kind of joy is not a discipline. This kind of joy comes from a passionate relationship with our Savior. This kind of joy is something that comes from within and flows outward. This kind of joy will cause more people to come to Jesus than anything else. People all over the world are looking for joy in drugs, success, things, drinking, fake relationships and much more. When the world sees the joy of Jesus in our lives people will be drawn and be curious about why we are so joyful. How about you? Do you walk in your first love for Jesus? Do you need to return to your first love? Do you know where you left your first love? Why not return to it today? Your friends and the world need to see the infectious joy you have for Jesus.

# Chapter 6
## ALL-OUT EVANGELISM

Michael Jordan went all out for basketball and became one of the greatest basketball players in the NBA. Tiger Woods went all out for golf and has been one of the world's greatest golfers. Steve Jobs went all out in the computer technology field and as head of the Apple Corporation became one of the greatest in his field. The list goes on.

What have you gone all out for? To what have you given your greatest focus and effort? What have you done with all your heart? If men and women can go all out in the arena of sports, medicine, technology and other fields, we should go all out for things that are eternal.

Outreach

Cold is good. Hot is good. Lukewarm is not good. Jesus expressed that in the book of Revelation.

*"I know all the things you do, that you are neither hot nor cold. I wish that you were one or the other! But since you are like lukewarm water, neither hot nor cold, I will spit you out of my mouth!"* Revelation 3:15-16 ( NLT)

Hot and cold is 'all out' from one extreme to the other, but lukewarm has not gone all out in any direction. I remember hearing a statement, 'if you don't stand for something you will fall for everything'. How true that is! If we don't go all out, we will not accomplish much in the Kingdom of God. People who want to lose weight or get into shape will not accomplish their goal unless they go all out. They cannot succeed unless they give it great attention and focus. Body builders are focused and intentional in what they are doing. If you and I are going to make a difference we must have the focus that causes us to go <u>all out</u>.

It seems to me that humanity is becoming less and less focused. It is almost like we have some kind of spiritual A.D.D. (Attention Deficit Disorder). It is like we are so bombarded by so much information that we can hardly focus on anything in a way that makes us effective. Jesus said, *"The light of the body is the eye: therefore **when thine eye is single**, thy whole body also is full of light."* Luke 11:34 (KJV)

Focus is the whole issue here. We need the kind of focus Jesus had when it came to reaching those who had yet come into a relationship with God. Jesus had laser-like focus. His focus was to seek and save those who were lost. *"For the Son of Man came to seek and to save what was lost."* Luke 19:10 (NIV)

All great men and women know how to maintain their focus. When I think of people like Hudson Taylor, George Whitfield, George Mueller, William Booth and others, these great leaders who left a mark that cannot be erased, were men who never lost their focus. We must, as believers who want to leave a mark that cannot be erased, develop a focus that is laser sharp.

A light that is extremely focused becomes a laser. The same light that you are enjoying as you read this book can become very focused and result in a laser that can cut through steel plate. We are the light of the world. Why not take the light that Jesus has already made us into, and get the same focus Jesus had for those who need to be saved, and become an effective laser in the Kingdom of God. I am sure you agree that Jesus' heart was for the lost to be saved. Yes, I totally believe in making disciples. Yet, without converts how do we continue to make disciples.

The world is in desperate need of people who want to see a change. The change believers want will not come through a political party, legislation, religious belief systems, more churches, or better preaching. If these things could bring change to our world, it would have already been transformed. God saw the answer from the foundations of the world. God sent His only Son; this is the answer for today. When people receive Jesus as their Lord and Savior, not only do they change but they become the conduit of change to their society. We must become the witnesses Jesus says we are. The world is ready. Are you?

The Institute for America Church Growth asked 10,000 people this question: What was responsible for your coming to Christ and this church? Their reply was:

## Get Motivated to Reach Your Friends

| | | |
|---|---|---|
| a. | I had a special need. | 3% |
| b. | I just walked in. | 3% |
| c. | I like the minister. | 6% |
| d. | I visited there. | 1% |
| e. | I like the Bible classes. | 5% |
| f. | I attended a gospel meeting. | 0.5% |
| g. | I like the programs. | 3% |
| **h.** | **A friend or relative invited me.** | **79%** |

The best time to reach people with the gospel is when they are new in a community or in a crises situation. I don't know if you are up-to-date on what is going on in the world, but God has the whole world in a crises situation. The whole world is in the best place it could be to receive the Gospel. The problem is we need people who will share the Good News when all they see on TV is bad news. Families are in crises, schools are in crises, the economy is in crises, our government is in crises and the church is in crises. Sounds like a good time to spread the Good News to me.

Teenagers today are the most unreached people for Christ in the nation. Less than 10 percent of America's youths have accepted Christ as their Lord and Savior. What we need is for God's people to go all out to reach people for Jesus. Andre' Crouch wrote a song in the 70's that still rings true.

*Jesus is the answer for the world today above Him there's no other, because Jesus is the way.*

The world has been set up by God for a massive harvest, but we need more laborers. *"Ask the Lord of the harvest, therefore, to send out workers into his harvest field."* Matthew 9:38

In the above verse, Jesus is asking for laborers because the world is ripe unto harvest. The problem is the same today. We are short on people who want to be harvesting souls for Jesus. The church needs to go all out for the same thing Jesus went all out for--people. God bankrupted heaven. He sent His only son. He did not hold anything back. God went all out for the salvation of people. What are we doing? I believe it is past time for the people of God to go all out with some hell-wrecking evangelism. It is past time for the sleeping giant (the church) to wake up.

*"And that, knowing the time, that now [it is] high time to awake out of sleep: for now [is] our salvation nearer than when we believed."* Romans 13:11 (KJV)

Evangelism must be taken off the back burner of many churches, and other churches need to get it back on the stove. When was the last time you obeyed Jesus and prayed for more harvesters in the fields that are white unto harvest? That's exactly what I mean.

We can gripe about the world situation or we can 'go all out' and win people to Jesus--that can change the world. I know griping is easier, I do some of that too. We need a wake-up call to evangelize our communities.

I have heard every excuse in the devil's book on why we are not obeying Jesus and reaching out to the world. Imagine a little girl drowning in a swimming pool with a lot of people standing around. Every one there sees the little girl is going under and coming up for a gasp of breath. Yet, the people just stand around saying things like:

1. Saving drowning people is not my gift.
2. I was not called into the ministry.
3. Ok everyone--pray.

4. I can't help, I am afraid of water.
5. She will be ok, someone else will save her.
6. What if I save her and she is turned away by my radicalness.

Evangelism is in every chapter of the book of Acts, except the 15th chapter. That is where they had a business meeting. If it was important to Jesus and to the apostles, maybe it should be important enough to us to do something about it? What are you thinking now? Only 2% of believers today share their faith regularly. There are so few North American Christians who practice sharing their faith that it takes 85 church members one full year to bring one person to faith in Jesus. The consequences of this lack are drastic, not only to the church but also to the lost world. We must, for the sake of our Lord, ourselves and the church, go all out in reaching the lost for Jesus. No holding back. No trying to be reserved. No trying to justify our complacency, no compromise and no excuses.

William Watley was the guest preacher at University Christian on July 10, 1988. His message,

Let's Go Outside, was one we all need to hear.  Let me share just one paragraph from the sermon.

*'It is no surprise that Jesus led the church outside, for His own ministry was an outside ministry.  Even when He was born there was no room for Him in the inn, so He was born outside in a stable.  He was not baptized in the temple but outside in the Jordan River by John the Baptist.  He was outside when the heavens opened up and a voice thundered forth which said, 'This is my beloved son with whom I am well pleased.'*

*He was outside when He delivered history's greatest message known as the Sermon on the Mount.  He was outside when (a woman) crawled through the crowd to touch the hem of His garment.  He was outside when He told the man who had lain beside the pool of Bethsaida for 38 years to 'Rise, take up your bed and walk. '  He was outside when He fed the five thousand with two fish and five barley loaves.  He was outside when He cured blind Bartamaeus.  He was outside when He was transformed on the mountain and Moses and Elijah stepped across the barriers of time and came and talked with Him.  He was outside when He called*

*Lazarus from the grave. He was outside when He calmed the raging storm. He was outside when He cleansed the 10 lepers. When He wanted to teach people about God's care for them He pointed outside and said, 'Consider the lilies of the field.....' He was outside of Gethsemane when He found out from His Father what was in the cup. And (He was outside) when He made the supreme sacrifice. Remember, Jesus was not crucified on an altar between two candlesticks, but outside on Golgotha's between two thieves.*

*And early that third day when they went to look for Him on the inside of the tomb the angels told them, 'He is not in here; He's outside for He is risen.' And when He got ready to ascend back to His Father, He led the church out as far as Bethany and stepped on a cloud. I don't know about you, but all the clouds I have seen are found outside. When He left, the angels told those gathered around that He's coming back again in the same manner that He parted from them outside.'*

If Jesus were here today, His plea would be to pray for more harvesters. My question is, "How do you pray for more harvesters if you are not willing to be a part of the answer." Evangelism will never happen by default, it will only happen by design. If something is going to happen in the area of evangelism in our lives or in the church it will not be by default. We must put forth the effort and design a strategy that will bring us into obedience in outreach. I don't want you to feel uncomfortable with these statements, but I want them to serve as a wake-up call. Christians go all out for a lot of good things. Let's make an 'all-out effort' to reach our communities and friends with the Good News that Jesus is real and wants to know them as friends.

I have something I would like for us to consider. Why does every church have a worship team, children's team, youth team, building team, finance team, yet so few churches have even thought of having an outreach team. I know that we develop teams for only those things that we feel are really important. Do you think evangelism is important to Jesus? Maybe we need to have a team. Later in the book I will explain the importance of a team and how to develop one.

I want us to see the heart of Paul the apostle.

*"To the Jews I became like a Jew, to win the Jews. To those under the law I became like one under the law (though I myself am not under the law), so as to win those under the law. To those not having the law I became like one not having the law (though I am not free from God's law but am under Christ's law), so as to win those not having the law. To the weak I became weak, to win the weak. I have become **all** things to **all** people so that **by all possible means** I might save some. I do **all** this for the sake of the gospel, that I may share in its blessings."* 1 Corinthians 9:20-23 (NIV)

I just love this verse! It really shows the Apostle Paul's heart when it comes to evangelism. His heart and concern was for all people to come to know Jesus. He did not care what it took to be able to share the gospel with people. He said I will become all things to all people to save some. Sharing the Good News with **all** people was a priority to the apostle Paul. It sounds like He went all-out. He said, 'that by all possible means....' Have you used all possible means to reach people? All possible means. That meant he did not hold back. He was not looking to find some theological balance. He went out with a passion to see people saved. In verse 2, Paul shares some great insight. He said, 'I do **all** this for the gospel's sake that I may share in its blessing'. WOW!!!! He becomes all things to all men that the gospel may be successfully spread. He did not care what it took to see people hear the gospel. Paul was not some religious jerk either. He became a Jew to the Jew and a Gentile to a Gentile. He did not put the Jews down for all their religious rules and rituals, nor did he put the Gentiles down. He went to share the gospel. You cannot be a jerk and win people to Jesus. Becoming all things to all people is a good way to be. This of course does not mean to do the things they do, but to fit in with them by being a friend--that will open a door and allow you to share. Jesus left heaven for us and became man to reach us. Paul had been so radically transformed by the power of the gospel he wanted to make sure everyone had the same chance he had. He knew the power of the gospel, because he had a personal encounter with Jesus on the road the Damascus that totally revolutionized his life. Perhaps we all need that kind of encounter--an encounter with Jesus that will put passion for others back in our hearts.

He also wanted to share in the blessing of the gospel: *'...that I may share in its blessing'*. I don't know about you, but I definitely want to share in the blessings of the gospel. The blessings of the gospel are more than can be mentioned in this book. Some of them are found in the blessing of going out and seeing the lives of others converted by the power of Jesus. Some of those blessings come as you take a step out of the boat and share Christ with someone and they break out in tears because of the hunger they had to hear the hope Jesus can give. Some of the blessing of the gospel is to see the power of God flow out of our lives as we get out of our comfort zone and share Christ with others. I think it is high time for you and me and the church to cash in on some of the blessings of the Gospel.

Peter said in 1 Peter 3:15, *"Be ready to speak up and tell anyone who asks why you're living the way you are, and always with the utmost courtesy."*

Be ready to speak up. Always looking for an opportunity to share how Jesus changed our lives and the reason we have the joy we have. This assumes people will see the difference in our lives. People should see something in us they desire.

Before I got saved, I had no interest in church at all. Part of the reason was the look on peoples' faces when they would go to church on Sunday morning. I remember watching people cross a street in Rosenberg Texas, to go to church on Sunday morning. They all looked so sad. I don't remember seeing any of them smiling, looking excited and giving each other high fives as they walked in to church. I remember feeling sorry for them. I would think, 'if only they had what I had. If I could just get them high or drunk, I could make them happy'. I could not understand why someone would go to church if they did not enjoy it. When I would go to bars and night clubs, we would meet each other in the parking lot, smiling, giving each other high fives and laughing. We knew we were fixing to have a great time.

For Peter to say 'we need to be ready to speak up and tell anyone who asks why we are living the way we are', suggests that we are living in a way that would cause people to ask. Come on, we need to let our lights shine so they ask. The unsaved world needs to look at us and see something that they desire. They need to see the difference. It's the difference that makes the difference. But always be courteous. In other words be nice to people. Never be rude or embarrass people. Treat people like Jesus would treat them. 1 Corinthians 15:58 tell us to go all out:

*"Therefore, my dear brothers and sisters, stand firm. Let nothing move you. Always give yourselves fully to the work of the Lord, because you know that your labor in the Lord is not in vain."*

Always give yourselves fully to the work of the Lord. How often? Not just on Sundays. Always. All the time be giving yourselves to the work of the Lord. Every day, all day, 24 hours a day, be employed by God. That sure fires me up.

At work today, give yourself to the work of the Lord. You can do that by being nice to someone. Let someone know you appreciate them. Hand them a nice gospel tract (we will talk about that later). There are hundreds of ways to give yourself to the work of the Lord. You don't have to preach, pastor, or be in any sort of leadership position. As a matter of fact you can be more effective by not being a pastor or preacher. That is why I work undercover most of the time. You can be effective by taking someone to lunch and becoming their friend. If you listen to what people are saying, they are usually reaching out. People today have lots of problems. Giving yourself to the work of the Lord is listening to others, loving others, being nice to others, and taking the opportunity when doors open up to you. You must use wisdom or you can turn people off. Just be genuine, caring and loving and you will have more opportunity than you could ever imagine.

Remember, the verse above said, *'because you know that your labor in the Lord is not in vain'*. Nothing is wasted in the Kingdom of God. Your efforts to reach others are always honored by God. Today, take the time to notice all the opportunities. Most of the time, we don't give ourselves fully to the work of the Lord, because we don't recognize all the opportunities available to us. If we did notice, we would be a lot nicer to people and not just hung up on ourselves. Try it today. You will be amazingly surprised. Get ready to give yourself fully to the work of the Lord. It will not be in vain.

# Chapter 7
# EFFECTIVENESS OF GOSPEL TRACTS

The church Michelle and I planted and pastored was extremely evangelistic. So the things you read in this book are not just things I dreamed up, but instead they have been proven by consistent practice. One year we baptized over 600 and averaged around 300 baptisms per year. If you sow you will reap. You cannot reap on a consistent basis if you do not sow on a consistent basis. Don't even expect to. Like a farmer who wants wheat but never plants, no matter how much he prays and intercedes, or even believes and confesses, he will not reap until he sows. Peter Lord, a good friend of mine, once said, "You can win a lot of ball games on the chalk board." Today people have a great plan, but it just stays on the chalk board and never gets on the field to be tried and proven. What you are reading is tried and proven, not just by me or the church I pastored but by many outreach churches that have reaped great harvests.

'The Gathering Church', the church my wife and I pastored for over 14 years, handed out 870,000 gospel tracts in a city of around 140,000 people. That comes to about 62,000 tracts per year, or 5,000 per month. Every living person in the area had about 6 tracts. We saturated our city with Gospel tracts. Each tract had the name of our church and our return address with a small place for someone to write their contact information and the decision they made. We received these tracts back from people who checked the box they had prayed to receive Christ.

These tracts came back from 21 different states in the USA and 5 different countries in the world. I think that gives gospel tracts some proven legitimacy. I know some people would say, 'How many of those decisions were real?' Who knows? But if one person was truly saved it was worth the effort, especially if that one was your son or daughter. How do you know if the decision of anyone who receives Christ, even at your church during an invitation, is real? The person who handed out the gospel tract was, at the very least, making an attempt to share Christ. When was the last time you made that attempt?

Tracts are not the only way of being obedient to sharing the gospel. It is a good way to get past fears and insecurities. It is a good starting place. I believe it is just one way to becoming an all-out kind of person. Tracts go back to Martin Luther, D.L. Moody, R.A Torrey, the Wesley brothers and many others of the great men of God. It is not something new, but something that has been effective for years and still is today. Tracts must be used with wisdom and compassion. There is a right way and a wrong way to do anything. Later in this chapter I will write about the right and effective way to use a tract. I personally have had thousands of great experiences using gospel tracts. I have also seen them used in ways that can turn a lost person away from Jesus. As believers we must use wisdom in everything we do.

*"I am sending you out like sheep among wolves. Therefore be as shrewd as snakes and as innocent as doves."* Matthew 10:16 (NIV)

I have been successfully using gospel tracts for the last 35 years. In this chapter I want to share some things about how to be effective using gospel literature.

It is important to know that when we use tracts, it is not just for the benefit of the person who receives the tract. Many, if not most of the time, it is for the benefit of the person who hands out the tract. Obedience always promotes spiritual growth. When someone attempts to obey the great commission (whether it is polished or unpolished) they are making an attempt to obey Jesus. This is always a good thing. Obedience gives birth to more obedience. Disobedience gives birth to more disobedience.

It is easy to fall into either one of these patterns. For example, giving finances to God. When someone obeys God in giving, they see God's faithfulness to honor their obedience. Then they want to obey Him more in the area of finances. When they see the blessings of Biblical giving it promotes more obedience in giving. When someone falls into hoarding their finances, by not giving, they fall into a pattern of working out all financial decisions in the flesh, without the help of God. They begin to lean on their own understanding. They miss out on seeing the miracles of God's supply. Disobedience then gives birth to more disobedience. Obedience becomes a way of life when a person begins to enjoy the benefits of obedience more than the issues that follow disobedience. The same principle works in the area of obeying God in outreach and evangelism.

*"I pray that you will be active in sharing what you believe. Then you will completely understand every good thing we have in Christ."* Philemon 4:6 (NIRV)

This is a very controversial passage. Some say it deals with evangelism-- some say it does not. I have spent much time researching this passage. Paul is encouraging Philemon to be active in sharing all that Christ has done for him. In the sharing of what Christ has done for him, he will in return come to a greater understanding of all the good things we have in knowing

Christ. The more we share of what Christ has done for us the more we come to a greater understanding of the riches we share in knowing Jesus. The passage seems to be saying that if we are not active in sharing our faith we cannot come to the knowledge of the good things we have in Christ. Obedience in sharing the Good News has incredible results.

It is so easy to just tell your story. Just share everything Jesus has done for you. Most people are more than willing to hear your story. Practice giving your testimony in five minute or less. Begin by telling your condition before you met Jesus. Be honest and don't exaggerate. Let them know what was happening in your life before you came to Jesus. Briefly tell the process of how you came to know Jesus. End it by stressing the difference He has made in your life and the benefits you enjoy today. This practice will not only bless the person you share with, but it will bring you into a greater knowledge of all the good things you have in Jesus. It may just remind you of all Jesus has done in your life. Go ahead and try this simple tool today. You can do it!

After sharing what Christ has done in your life, wouldn't it be great to leave some literature that simply repeats what you just shared including a few scripture references. This is the purpose of a Gospel tract. When you hand a tract to someone, let them know that the little pamphlet has a return address on it so if they decide to give their hearts to Christ they can put a stamp on it. Then someone will mail them materials on how to grow spiritually. It is like a Christian's business card. For years I did not carry business cards. Instead I would give a gospel tract that had my contact information on it. It will amaze you how many positive responses you get from people, especially when you use them in the right way--with a good spirit and attitude.

I also try to take the opportunity to pray with people when I hand them one of my gospel tracts. Do this in a way that will not embarrass them. If they are around their friends I usually will not ask. If you get the opportunity to pray with someone, you will find they deeply appreciate it. I find most people in the world believe in prayer, some more than those in the church. Usually I will say something like this, "Listen, before I go, is there something you would like to see God do in your life? Would you mind if I pray for you right now?" Get ready, most are willing for you to pray for them. Don't pray a long prayer. Be brief. Show that you genuinely care. Let them know you care by telling them. Remember, people don't care how much you know, until they know how much you care. If you can, get a phone number so you can call and check on them at a later time. Let them know you will not bother them; you just want to check to see if God had answered the prayer. Be real! It is so nice when you leave to know that you left a tract so if they decide to commit their heart to Christ sometime in the future, they can mail the card in and you can follow-up. I cannot tell you how many times this has happened to me.

I design my own gospel tracts and have for years. Generic tracts just don't communicate my heart and soul, or say what I want to say in a non-religious manner. When I write and design a tract, I try to think like a person who has no interest in Church or Christianity. I try to use words that will connect with them. You may want to design a tract for the kind of person you want to target. Or you can design a general one that is effective for all people. Below is just one of the many tracts I have designed. A tract should not say too much. You want a small seed to get them thinking. Too much print will turn them off. I am a believer and too much print turns me off.

## Sample tract

Friend

Friendship is having someone who you can trust; someone you can tell your darkest secrets to and not be rejected. It's having someone you can talk to about anything, anytime. This is the type of friendship we long for, yet it seems to be the one thing we can't find. Still, we search for it and get "burned" by our relationships.

loved

Human love has a way of doing that to us. But God's love for you is not human love. God's love is divine. Human love needs something that will capture its attention. Therefore, we are always trying to perform and meet expectations to win certain people over. Human love is always reaching out to fill a gap that only God's love can fill.

accepted

God's love needs nothing in return. First John says that "God is love." He doesn't love you because you go to church or give money or act a certain way. He knows that doing all of the "right things" will come naturally when you have a relationship with Him. You can trust Him, tell Him anything without fear of rejection, and talk to Him anytime and any place. He just loves you!

safe

Why not give Jesus a chance? He'll never reject you. Just open your heart to Him. He's waiting and will hear your prayer. Pray something like the prayer below and mean it in your heart, then fill out this card and mail it to us. We'll send you some material to help you know Him better. The Good News is you can Connect with Jesus; a True Friend.

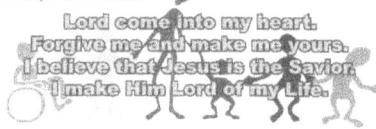

Lord come into my heart.
Forgive me and make me yours.
I believe that Jesus is the Savior.
I make Him Lord of my Life.

*If you prayed this prayer, please fill out the back of this card and drop it in the mail and we will send you a booklet with information to help you on your new journey.*

## Another one

The idea behind a gospel tract is to get their attention. You have a very small window of time to accomplish that. First impression is everything. You only get one chance to have a first impression. So make it good. The front of the tract must be impressive and a great attention getter. Whether you write your own or use a generic one, the idea here is to get engaged in connecting people and Jesus. Don't make this one of those games you win on a chalk board. When you start using tracts, you will immediately notice a change in your own spiritual life. Remember, it does as much for you as the person you witness to.

There are many ways and approaches to witness to people. Using tracts is just one way of many. I have always considered handing a tract to someone as an initial way of getting people started in outreach. My evangelism experience of over 35 years has taught me many things. One thing is that people usually have to start in the shallow end before they dive off in the deep end. Very few people start their outreach experience by walking into a restaurant, getting a prophetic word or a word of wisdom for the waitress/waiter, and then sharing that word which then leads them to Jesus right there and then. Few, if any, walk in that same restaurant, pray over a sick person that gets healed and saved that evening. Those things do happen and should happen on a regular basis.

What I want to teach in this book is a simple approach that anyone can use. You can be very shy, introverted, or totally inexperienced in outreach. Using a tract is just a good place to get started. It will make you aware of the many outreach opportunities we have every day. Using tracts will bring you into an evangelism awareness. Even if you are really shy, the next time you go to a clothing store, just put a tract in a pair of blue jeans on the rack. Someone will purchase those jeans take them home and get the gospel. You never know what will happen to that tract. The teenager could take the tract out and lay it down somewhere at home. Then mom could read it, or a brother or sister could read it and get saved. You just never know. By placing a tract in that pocket you witnessed to someone. Doing that is a lot better than doing nothing. Do you agree? If the tract ended up in the trash at least you got out of your comfort zone and attempted to share the gospel. That makes Jesus happy. The more you practice handing tracts to people or putting them in the restroom, the more you will become evangelistic as a life-style. I have a good time just finding fun places to put tracts.

Public restrooms are a great place. Most people are looking for some reading literature while they are there. So they conveniently find your gospel tract there on top of the toilet paper holder. Guess what most people will do while resting there. Read it. That's a seed planted. I like to roll the tract up in the toilet paper. It is a real surprise. Sometimes when I go to a public restroom, and no one else is in there, I will put a tract in every stall. I think fishing for men can be fun. Michelle and I used to get applications for credit cards almost every week. You know the ones I am talking about. The ones with the self-addressed, postage paid envelopes. We would put a tract in the postage paid envelope and put it in the mail with-out the credit card application. Someone has to open the envelope. Maybe they are facing something in their life that will cause them to read it. You never know. It is a seed planted. On Halloween, I designed a cool looking gospel tract for that particular evening. Then our youth would go 'tract or treating'. It is a great time to knock on doors. Everyone else is.

    Tracts can be effective and fun. Most importantly, it is causing you to think about reaching people and getting you used to being out of your comfort zone. Many times when I check out at a store I will smile real big, be very nice, and tell them I have something that will really encourage them. I hand them a tract and ask them if they would read it on their break. Then I joke with

## Outreach

them and ask them when I walk away if they are going to trash it. I laugh and they usually laugh, but they promise me they will read it. I just planted a seed.

You can also place a tract in every bill you send in the mail. Keep a stack of them where you write your checks and pay your bills. Remember, all of this will do more for you spiritually than anyone else. It is a great spiritual exercise. If no one gets saved reading your tracts, you will be changed from your obedience to the Great Commission. Handing out a tract may not seem like much, but it is better than nothing. If tracts were effective for people like R.A. Torrey, Martin Luther, D.L. Moody, and Billy Graham, they are still effective for people today. I have meet many worship leaders, pastors and other people who shared with me how they got saved reading a gospel tract. I am sure they are glad someone used them. Let's not be critical of any kind of evangelism, God can use anything.

Even when I do servant evangelism, I try to give people a tract. Not only does it have my ministry address to follow up if they mail it in, but it has a seed in it that could get planted in their heart. There are two very important things that make handing out tracts effective:

1. **What the tract presents.** It must be a loving and brief presentation. That is why I always design and write my own. It needs to present Jesus as Someone who really loves and cares about them. Everyone is looking for love. A tract needs to have a ministry name or a church name on it with a return address. This way they have an idea that it is not some flakey, far out, weird person who is passing them out. That is why I generally like to hand them to someone personally. I try to befriend them in the short time that I have before I hand the tract to them. When the tract is returned to you in the mail, be sure to mail them some discipleship material. If they put their email address, send them a short note of congratulations. If they respond to your email, then try to hook them up to a Bible preaching, teaching church that will be friendly. This one could take some time on your part.

2. **How you present the tract.** "...*for the kingdom of God is not eating and drinking, but righteousness and peace and joy in the Holy Spirit...*" Romans 14:7. Joy is

critical to evangelism. It is hard to express to people the incredible benefits of knowing Jesus when you look like you have the flu. Remember, we have Good News. Joy is such an impressive fruit of the Spirit when you are trying to reach people. The expression on our faces should be one of genuine, authentic joy. If you put on a fake expression it shows to the lost world. The world has a way of telling if we are real or fake. As I have said before, being real is extremely important to reaching people today. You don't want some goofy smile, but one of joy and satisfaction. Just be you with joy.

Be caring when you present a tract to someone. Without Christ people go to hell forever. This always gives me a real concern for them. The eyes are the window of the heart. If you really care about someone, they can see it in your eyes. No matter what their response is, always be loving and caring with joy in your heart. People are not our enemy. Satan wants us to dislike the lost because of how they act. Lost people act like lost people. Don't let the enemy win a victory by turning your heart against people who do not know

Jesus. Jesus loved you and me even while we were yet sinners. Even if someone is rude when you present a tract, you reply by being very loving and kind. I have had very few people act rudely to me when I hand them a tract. This is because of how I present myself. I use humor, kindness and love. People usually respond very positively to this kind of attitude.

Tracts serve as a reminder for us to share Jesus with people. It is easy to get caught up in being busy and not thinking about the opportunities we have to share Jesus with others. Our focus can get off easily in our busy world. Yet, having a Gospel tract in our possession serves as a reminder where our focus should be.

A friend of mine, Arthur Blessit, uses bright red Jesus stickers. He has carried the cross in every nation and every island in the world handing out his bright red Jesus stickers. Find something that works for you if tracts and Jesus stickers do not. Whatever you do, step into obedience and start spreading the gospel.

Outreach

# Chapter 8
## CATCH AND RELEASE

It is one thing to be able to catch fish, but it is another to keep them alive after you catch them. I know some professional fisher men who catch fish for fun -- only to throw them back. This was not what Jesus had in mind. Jesus' command was to 'make disciples'. Evangelism is only successful when we catch them and keep them. I know of some churches who brag about how many fish they caught in a year, but so few ever lived. There is a real art to catching and keeping them alive. I want to share some very practical ways of keeping them alive to disciple. These methods are not infallible and can and should be modified to fit different churches and groups. As a pastor and evangelist, I have tried and proven these methods over many years.

Discipleship does not just happen. It takes a major effort and a well-oiled strategy.

*"Suppose one of you wants to build a tower. Will he not first sit down and estimate the cost to see if he has enough money to complete it?"* Luke 14:28 (NIV)

Jesus' command was for us to 'make disciples'. I like the word 'make'. This implies something that we must do. It does not just happen. In my own life, had it not been for Jerry (the person who led me to the Lord and stayed with me afterward) I would never have made it as a believer. It was because of his effort (and it took a lot) that I was discipled.

Having a team and a well- oiled plan makes no progress unless you work the plan. Remember, you can win a lot of ball games on a chalk board. You have to have a plan, and then work the plan. Hundreds of churches have a plan for follow - up, but the follow-up plan basically was ineffective. We need a plan that works, one that has been proven and has borne fruit. A plan like this brings success that will help motivate you to continue the plan and tweak it to make it even better. A good plan is simple and does not require too much effort on the part of the person doing the follow up.

The people on your team should be those who really want to get to know the new believers, in order to disciple them. Ideally, this should be all the people in church who love Jesus and likewise love their neighbors. This should be people who want to obey the great commission of going and making disciples. Notice we have to go and do the making, God does not do the disciple making; He left that for us to accomplish. We all need a burden for new babies in Jesus. Too many times people are abandoned just like in the real world where moms abandon their own children in trash dumpsters and door steps. We need to love our mission and have a plan to work that mission. If it is the whole church that wants to accomplish the Great Commission, the team will need to be the catalyst that will impart the DNA of evangelism into the Body of Christ. People will see the joy the team is having reaching people for Jesus and seeing new people growing in truth. There are three things that really work when it comes to catching and keeping the new believers. I call this connecting to the new believer. Here are the three things that have been proven to work.

## 1. CALL

Someone on the evangelism team needs to head up the team that CONNECTS with each new convert. This needs to be someone who is very pleasant on the phone and has common sense when it comes to making short phone calls. The leader of this team should start by strategically selecting a few people to be on her team. This will also begin to grow your evangelism team which means more people in the church start getting excited about seeing people saved and discipled.

When someone makes a profession of faith, they need to receive a call. It should be short and friendly. Let them know how glad you are they made a decision to follow Jesus. Invite them back to church and make sure they got the discipleship book handed to them after they prayed to receive Jesus. (I also have written a workbook specifically for new converts. This can be ordered on our web site (donbabin.com). Do not overwhelm them by telling them all the programs the church has to help them. Just be a friend to them. Inquire about their job, family, etc. Make sure they know how happy you are about the new life they are going to have in Jesus. Encourage them to work a little each evening in the workbook that was given to them. Leave them your phone number so they can call if they have any questions. Tell them you will be looking for them next Sunday.

2. **CARD**

After the phone call the same person needs to write a card of encouragement. You can purchase these at a book store or have the church print their own. Timing is the key effectiveness. The card needs to be written the same Sunday as the phone call and their profession of faith. We want them to know we genuinely care about them and want to make sure they mature after their decision. Think about this: someone makes a profession of faith, they are welcomed by the church and they see the joy the church has over their profession of faith and are given a work book to help them grow in their decision. That afternoon they get a phone call from someone who is not on staff or paid to call them. The person calling is genuinely excited and wants to help. Then on Tuesday (depending on your mail service) they receive an encouraging post card from the same person who called. The card also has the phone number of the person who called and wrote the card. This person will begin to get the idea that someone really cares.

## 3. CONTACT

This is where a discipleship relationship can begin. Jesus commands all of us to make disciples. To fully follow Jesus we MUST be in the process of making disciples. Transformation will happen in both the discipler and the disciple while walking in obedience to the Great Commission,

*"Then the eleven disciples went to Galilee, to the mountain where Jesus had told them to go. When they saw him, they worshiped him; but some doubted. Then Jesus came to them and said, "All authority in heaven and on earth has been given to me. Therefore go and make disciples of all nations, baptizing them in the name of the Father and of the Son and of the Holy Spirit, and*

*teaching them to obey everything I have commanded you. And surely I am with you always, to the very end of the age."* Matthew 18:16 - 20

The perfect scenario is that the person who hands the convert the book also makes the phone call within 24 hours. The same person then writes the card and welcomes them and lets the new believer know someone cares. This same person should meet them a little before church or some other place to see how they are doing and check on the progress they are making on the follow-up booklet. Just imagine this being you. At a service at church you pray to receive Christ. A person with a great smile and a compassionate heart welcomes you and gathers some information from you and hands you a workbook to help you in your new walk with Jesus. The same person calls you later that day to check on you and see if you have any questions. Then on Tuesday you receive a card in the mail. This makes the whole process about relationship which helps you succeed in your new walk with Jesus.

When we disciple someone, we will discover a large part of our spiritual purpose. I think the process should start slowly. People are basically slow to develop relationships and are almost paranoid. The first meeting should be a tag-on meeting at church or a short meeting at a coffee shop or something like that. It should not be a long meeting, just a chance to get to know each other. Being too pushy can run people off.

As a brief review, let me go over the main elements of maintaining the catch. The person gets a follow up booklet from a member at the church where they receive Christ as Lord and Savior. Then the process begins. They get a phone call within 24 hours. A post card arrives in the mail within 3-4 days after their decision. Then they meet together for a short meeting to review the progress in the workbook.

These steps are very simple and not time consuming ideas. They have been proven over many years. Not only will it be a vital part of the new believer's life, but it will be life changing for the one doing the follow up.

# Chapter 9
# SERVANT EVANGELISM

Mobilizing people to reach the lost has been my passion since the mid-seventies. I think I have tried every imaginable and ethical way to motivate people to care about those who do not know Jesus and are headed to a Christ-less eternity. This has been one of the most difficult tasks Jesus has assigned to my life. Upon the discovery of 'Servant Evangelism', I found a way that every person, no matter what their spiritual gifting or personality type, can participate and be successful. Servant Evangelism is a way that all can enjoy and be effective while fulfilling the great commission. I have taught churches the "how-to's" and have seen great results. Almost all who participate in this type of outreach have shared the excitement and peace that follows from doing what Jesus has commanded all of us to do.

The joy each person gets from following our Lords command to 'GO' is indescribable. We always end our church-wide servant evangelism outreaches with testimonies. The most exciting part of the day is hearing the children of God excited about how they affected their community by obeying Jesus. Every church can be a part of touching their communities. This chapter is one of the most exciting chapters in the book because it will help you can learn how to mobilize people to take part in affecting not just the believers in church but touching the un-churched right there in your community.

Jesus said to be great we must be servants:

*"Jesus called them together and said, 'You know that the rulers of the Gentiles lord it over them, and their high officials exercise authority over them. Not so with you. Instead, whoever wants to become great among you must be your servant...'"* Matthew 20:25-26

Let me begin by explaining about servant evangelism. Servant Evangelism is loving people in a way that love becomes real and tangible. I believe the unbelieving world is tired of being told but not shown. Whenever we show people acts of kindness (servant evangelism) they see Christianity in action. Loving people always works. Servant evangelism is about giving something away that meets an immediate need. It is never accepting anything in return, but simply showing people that we care. I have been amazed at the world's response to showing love in a practical way. When we humble ourselves to serve, people do not view us as know-it-alls or snooty Christians.

Serving and loving people have miraculous effects. I think Jesus knew the way to touch people's hearts was to serve them in love. I have been involved in evangelistic outreaches for over 37 years, but when I started serving people from a heart of love, it not only changed the people I served but it has had tremendous effect on me. Seeing the shock on people's faces as you smile at them and hand them a bottle of water, or coins at a car wash, is the most wonderful experience you will ever have serving Jesus and others. No matter what I have given away to serve people, they always say, "Why are you doing this?" I love seeing their faces when I respond, 'This is just a cool way of showing you the love of Jesus." Many times they don't even know how to answer.

We live in a world where everyone is trying to get something from you or take something from you. When someone gives something away with a big smile on their face, it stuns people. No matter what spiritual gifting we have, we should all, from the youngest to the oldest, be serving others if we want to be great in the Kingdom of God.

When I think about Jesus in the New Testament, I think of someone who was humble and loving. This is what made him so approachable to all people. Jesus genuinely cared about people. This is very different from where the church is today. I do not know about you, but I want people to see Jesus in me. There was a song that was real popular in the 80's that said, 'you may be the only Jesus that people see'. When I think about those words, I can't help but think, 'what kind of Jesus is the world seeing today?' Don't you want to do your best, by the power of the Holy Spirit, to present to the world the Jesus of the New Testament? Jesus was nice. Jesus was loving. Jesus was humble and lowered himself to be a servant. This is what servant evangelism is based on. Here's how it works.

One of my favorite forms of servant evangelism is handing out cool bottles of waters on a hot day. Anyone can hand someone a bottle of cool water on a hot day. When we take out a group outside the doors of the church building to love the community we always teach them the basics. Things like never wear sun glasses.

We want people to see our eyes. Eyes are the windows of the heart. Your eyes can show a happy joyful heart. Another basic part of one of our outreaches is to have a lot of fun. It is critical that the world see Christians having fun serving them and serving Jesus.

The world notices joy. One day I was driving in Houston, Texas, and as I approached a red light there was a person washing car windows and asking for donations. He looked homeless and needy. My first thought was that I did not want to give one more person standing at the corner any money. But this person was different. I watched him as I drove closer to the corner where he was working. He was washing car windshields. He was smiling from ear to ear, dancing around and laughing. He was having the greatest time entertaining each person that drove by. When I got to his corner I allowed him to wash my window and gladly gave him a dollar. I was so impressed with the joy and fun he was having I was glad to help him out. Another example is a Chinese restaurant I use to go to. The owner was a lady that had such joy in what she did. When I would go inside she always came to my table and was smiling from ear to ear. She would let me know how glad she was to see me. She made me feel like she really wanted me to come eat there so we could visit. She would even bring me an appetizer, and tell me it was on her. Her kindness made me want to go back and eat there. The food was not that good at all, but her joy and kindness was what made me want to support her restaurant. This is a lesson the church could learn.

FREE WATER. We also have a sign with the name of the church. We do this because people are very suspicious and when we identify ourselves they are not as skeptical. Spread the people out down the street so as the car approaches people can read each sign. When they stop at the red light, you will be smiling and having a lot of fun. You simply ask them if they would like a bottle of free water. We also have a business card or gospel tract and hand that to them with the bottle of water. We always try to hand them something with a short gospel message and the name of the church doing the outreach.

The reason we want to give them something with the gospel on it is we want them to know it is the Christian church that is showing them love. Also, image just giving out water and no gospel. What if they die that day and never got to read the gospel. Then we just sent them to hell with their thirst quenched. It is important that the name of the church or the organization is identified so if they want to know more, they have the information they need.

We do most of our outreaches on a Saturday morning. Not too early so people who want to can sleep in that day. We never do an outreach that lasts over two hours. We want people to come out, have fun, reach out to people by loving them and serving them, yet get home in time to do what they need to do. If you meet at the church, or some other location, at around 9:30, do some brief training, do some role play, pray and head out. Finish by 11:30 and go back to church to have some testimonies, then everyone one will get home at a decent time. If people realize they can do something like this once a month, for just a couple of hours, and still get done what they need to get done on a Saturday, you increase your possibility of more people helping out.

We always have someone taking pictures and shooting some video. This way, on Sunday morning you can have a short presentation of all the fun you had and even have a few testimonies from those who participated. This is always a great time. When others hear their friends sharing stories, and see the joy on their faces, they will want to join your next outreach.

We frequently hear testimonies of people who cannot believe how easy it was and the fun they had. We also hear testimonies of those who we have served.

Sometimes we go to Laundromats and given away bottles of water and a gospel tract, and we put the quarters in the washer or dryer. As we put the quarters in they always ask, "Why are you doing this?" We love to tell them that we are doing this to show people the love of Jesus in a very practical way. They are blown away. We try to ask everyone if there is something they would like to see God do for them. This is much better than asking them if there is something they would like for us to pray for them about. When we ask them if there is something they would like God to do for them, we get a better response. You will be shocked at the responses. I have seen grown men break down and cry because of the love we have shown them, and then we pray with them. I wish every believer could be a part of this. The church is really missing out by not doing what Jesus said to do, 'GO'.

To be successful, with lots of people participating, you must have at least 3 -4 weeks of promo on Sunday mornings before the outreach. I suggest finding some video on You Tube; we even have a few videos of our outreaches on You Tube. Show them on Sunday morning so folks know what to expect. Have a short skit of what you will be doing. Make it fun and show lots of love and joy.

I suggest you do a search on Google on servant evangelism. There is so much material out there. All I wanted to do with this chapter is to 'whet your appetite' and let you see a different type of reach out. Happy Serving!

# MY STORY

The memories of my early life begin during the hippie generation. My preteen and teen years were surrounded by rock & roll, rebellion, drugs, alcohol, unrestrained sex. I went along with a generation of youth who had lost all sense of responsibility. Life was a wild party. My heroes were Jimmy Hendrix, Led Zeppelin, Janice Joplin, The Rolling Stones and other radical rock and rollers. My life, from about age 12 through 21, was lived with no restraints. I don't want to glorify my past or give it any more lime light then necessary, but use it to show you the difference Jesus can make in someone who is willing to TOTALLY surrender to Him.

I drank alcohol like crazy and did enough drugs to kill many people. I did them all: heroin, LSD, mescaline, speed, downers, cocaine, heroin mixed with cocaine (commonly called speedballs), smoked pot, peyote, hash, ate mushrooms and anything else that would get me high.

I was shooting up drugs like a crazy man. I had been arrested in Richmond, Texas (three times), Freeport, Texas, Ruidoso, New Mexico, and Westwego, Louisiana (close to New Orleans -- for possession with the intent to sell drugs, public intoxication, assault and battery, and other stupid things).

All I cared about was being high or drunk. I did not care about anyone including myself. I was lost, confused, and full of anger and hate. Many times I would ask myself why I was born. I had no idea what true love was, or what it would be like to be loved unconditionally or to love someone unconditionally. Self was the center of my life. I felt like I would never get old and never die. I felt invincible, fearless, and I did not live beyond the next party. I had no idea what the future held for me, nor did I care.

As a student I was rebellious, lazy, did not care to study or apply myself at all. I did not care about graduating from high school, but a friend talked me into staying to the end. I did graduate, but only after being run out of one school and sent to another one in

Rosenberg, Texas. I hated school, authority, teachers, rules, laws and anyone who got in my way.

My rebellion and my way of life deeply affected my relationship with my parents. I expected them to allow me to run free. Since they gave me a hard time for staying out late, and sometimes not even coming home, I started hating them. I felt like they just stood in the way of my doing what I wanted to do, and how long I wanted to do it, and when I wanted to do what I wanted to do. This caused much conflict in our home, as you can imagine. There was always tension and fighting among us. I know now, but did not know then, that I broke their hearts in millions of little pieces. I was so drunk on myself that I did not even realize the pain I had created in their lives.

So here I was. A drug addict, drinking all the time, in and out of jail, over- dosing on drugs, waking up in hospitals due to drug over- doses, full of hate, rebellion, drunk on myself, and destroying my family.

After getting out of jail, needless to say I was getting pretty sick of myself and my lifestyle. I had no idea there was a way to change. I grew up Catholic and most of what happened in church back then was in Latin. So I had no idea about what God could do. I had no idea what the gospel was about. Lost, helpless, confused and not knowing how to change, all I knew was there was no way I could change myself.

One night a friend and I were out shooting drugs and drinking tequila, and we ended up at my brother's apartment in Houston, Texas. We shot so much heroin that night my friend died, with my belt tied around his arm and my needle stuck in his vein. I was so messed up, I had to crawl a couple of blocks on my hands and knees to get help. I told myself I would never do drugs again-- only to start right back up two days later. I had no idea if there was even a way to be set free.

BUT GOD!!!! I love those words. You find them all the way through the Bible. I had my, BUT GOD moment. I was headed to hell, did not care if I ended up there, and was taking many people with me. I had been busted for drugs and a stolen car in Westwego, Louisiana. I was able to leave the state of Louisiana on a special bond and go back to Texas to wait for my trial. It looked like I was going to have to do time in prison. I started getting scared, for the first time in my life. I was young and did not want to go to the penitentiary. I started feeling like I wasn't invincible. Despite all this, when I got back to Texas I went right back to drugs and alcohol. At this time I was doing large quantities of many narcotics. I was a serious addict.

It was at this low point of my life that I had my "BUT GOD" moment. It was here that someone started sharing the gospel with me. I had no idea what 'born again' was. Those words were not popularized until the Jimmy Carter presidency. Jerry, an old high school friend who I used to party with, began to witness to me. I was stunned that this friend was into the Jesus stuff. Jesus was pretty much all he talked about. He would always tell me how he was 'born again', and that I needed to be saved.

I thought Jerry had gone crazy. I really did. I thought that he possibly did too many drugs and fried his brain. I even started feeling sorry for him. I thought that he had been hanging out with some religious folks that had brain washed him and ruined a perfectly good drug addict. I did all I could to get him to turn back to drugs and start getting high again. Nothing I said or did had any effect on him. This really made an impression on me. I began to see that whatever this Jesus stuff was all about it definitely could change a life. Jerry witnessed to me like I was going to die and go to hell that day. Every time I saw him he told me about Jesus. I would listen but did not want him to think I was. I wanted what he had, but I did not want to give up drugs, sex, rock and roll or anything else. I wanted to have my life changed, but I still loved all the things I was doing.

Jerry shared the gospel with me for over a year. Listen to me! Don't ever give up on a friend. You never know when your words will take effect. Little by little, what Jerry was saying was getting through. Finally, he invited me to a revival service and I told him I would go. I must admit I was scared to death. I had no idea what people did inside of those church buildings. What I knew about church came from the expressions on people's faces as they walked in and out of the church building. I must say, they were not happy or excited. When we would go to a bar and see our friends, we would be happy and giving each other high fives. Now the church people gave a completely different picture. They looked like someone had to beat them into going. This really scared me. All I knew was my friend met Jesus and church had something to do with it. It was only because of the difference I saw in Jerry that I was willing to go with him. In the back of my mind I really wanted what Jerry had, but I figured there was no way God could or would do that for me. If only I could have what Jerry had and still do drugs and get drunk. The message Jerry shared with me was about total abandonment to Jesus. I wasn't sure I could do that.

      Jerry came to pick me up to take me to church. (I learned later this is a Christian strategy to make sure the person you want to go to church doesn't talk himself out of going.) That night was the first time I had heard a preacher share the gospel. The whole service was culture shock. I was looking for a rock band or something but instead there was a 78 year old grey-headed lady playing the piano. They sang songs that I had never heard in my life. Everybody had a little catalogue full of songs supplied to them in little catalogue holders in each pew. As I looked at the bottom of the page of each song I noticed dates like 1879, 1797, and others. I thought it was the golden oldie song book. Then, at the bottom of one page, I saw the date 1902. WOW, a new one. I remember thinking that these people had not seen a song writer saved in a long time.

When the evangelist preached, I was absolutely shocked. I had never heard anything like this in my life. He yelled, screamed, ran from one side of the stage to the other, and spat on everyone on the front row. Watching him gave me whip lash. He would look over at me and say, "You have been doing drugs and drinking and need a change". I remember getting so angry at Jerry for telling the preacher all my sin. When the invitation came the Holy Spirit was all over me. The evangelist said, "One more verse and we will stop the invitation." That was a lie because they sang those verses over and over. Finally, I got up from my seat and went to the front to receive Jesus as my Lord and Savior.

My "BUT GOD" moment started the miracles. God miraculously delivered me from all drug and alcohol addiction. I immediately stopped smoking cigarettes. I had to stop listening to rock music because it was such a 'god' to me and an influence I was not strong enough to deal with. At this time another miracle happened. My trial was canceled and I was set free from any charges against me in Louisiana.

God gave me an incredible hunger for His word. I read all the time. It was like I could never get enough of His word. That hunger is still with me to this day. Praying became a vital part of each day of my life, and still is today. The miracle God did in my life is beyond explanation. He called me to preach the gospel. He gave me a beautiful wife and later two of the most incredible and awesome sons, Dustin & Carman. WOW!! God did all this because He really loved me.

I started learning and am still learning today about God's unconditional love. This is life changing. He has allowed me to travel across America and preach the gospel as a full time evangelist for over sixteen years. We founded and pastored a church for fourteen years, and now serve as missionary/evangelists to the Maasai tribe in East Africa. My wife, Michelle, has stood by my side and served Jesus right along with me for these many years.

I would be in hell today if it were not for my friend, Jerry, who took the great commission seriously and loved me enough to share Jesus with me. My wife and I have been privileged to see over 100,000 professions of faith in the USA and other countries of this world. There are many other Don Babins out there but so few Jerrys. Why won't you be the next Jerry. Why don't you stand up for Jesus and obey Him and let your light shine. Try getting out of your salt-shaker Christianity and start shaking and shinning for Jesus. Let's take this Jesus thing more seriously and get out of our comfort zones and become mad men for Jesus. He loves you doesn't want you to be ashamed of Him. He loves you and wants the world to know this love too. It is time for you to GO!!!!

*This is a very brief version of what God did in my life. To obtain a DVD of My Story, go to [donbabin.com](donbabin.com) and download a copy.*

www.ingramcontent.com/pod-product-compliance
Lightning Source LLC
Chambersburg PA
CBHW071923290426
44110CB00013B/1450